Beyond the Periphery of the Skin

T0125608

KAIROS

In ancient Greek philosophy, *kairos* signifies the right time or the "moment of transition." We believe that we live in such a transitional period. The most important task of social science in time of transformation is to transform itself into a force of liberation. Kairos, an editorial imprint of the Anthropology and Social Change department housed in the California Institute of Integral Studies, publishes groundbreaking works in critical social sciences, including anthropology, sociology, geography, theory of education, political ecology, political theory, and history.

Series editor: Andrej Grubačić

Recent and featured Kairos books:

Re-enchanting the World: Feminism and the Politics of the Commons by Silvia Federici

Birth Work as Care Work: Stories from Activist Birth Communities by Alana Apfel

Occult Features of Anarchism: With Attention to the Conspiracy of Kings and the Conspiracy of the Peoples by Erica Lagalisse

Anthropocene or Capitalocene? Nature, History, and the Crisis of Capitalism edited by Jason W. Moore

We Are the Crisis of Capital: A John Holloway Reader by John Holloway

Archive That, Comrade! Left Legacies and the Counter Culture of Remembrance by Phil Cohen

Autonomy Is in Our Hearts: Zapatista Autonomous Government through the Lens of the Tsotsil Language by Dylan Eldredge Fitzwater

The Battle for the Mountain of the Kurds: Self-Determination and Ethnic Cleansing in the Afrin Region of Rojava by Thomas Schmidinger

Building Free Life: Dialogues with Öcalan edited by International Initiative

For more information visit www.pmpress.org/blog/kairos/

Beyond the Periphery of the Skin

Rethinking, Remaking, and Reclaiming the Body in Contemporary Capitalism

Silvia Federici

BTL

KAIROS

PM

Beyond the Periphery of the Skin: Rethinking, Remaking, and Reclaiming the Body in Contemporary Capitalism
Silvia Federici
© 2020 PM Press.

ISBN: 978-1-62963-706-8
Library of Congress Control Number: 2019933013

Cover image by Silvia Federici (1971)
Cover by John Yates / www.stealworks.com
Interior design by briandesign

10 9 8 7 6 5 4 3 2

PM Press
PO Box 23912
Oakland, CA 94623
www.pmpress.org

Autonomedia
PO Box 568 Williamsburg Station
Brooklyn, NY 11211-0568 USA
info@autonomedia.org
www.autonomedia.org

This edition first published in Canada in 2020 by Between the Lines
401 Richmond Street West, Studio 281, Toronto, Ontario, M5V 3A8,
Canada
1-800-718-7201
www.btlbooks.com

ISBN 978-1-77113-487-3

Canadian Cataloguing in Publication information available from
Library and Archives Canada

Printed in the USA.

Contents

PART THREE

PART FOUR

Acknowledgments

Beyond the Periphery of the Skin owes its existence to an invitation, in 2015, by the Anthropology and Social Change Department that is housed in the California Institute of Integral Studies, to deliver three lectures on the theme of the body that were then to be published by PM Press. This gave me the opportunity to not only rethink themes that have been central to my work but also to collect in one volume past articles devoted to this subject. My first thanks, then, go to the director of the Anthropology and Social Change Department, Andrej Grubačić, and to PM Press.

I also want to thank the women creators of the "Free Home University," who participated in a workshop that was held in my home town, Parma, Italy, June 11–16, 2019, on the question of the body and social reproduction, with whom I read and discussed the articles forming Part One of this book. I thank especially Gaia Alberti, Sarah Amsler, Edith Bendicente, Carla Bottiroli Greil, Claire Doyon, Daria Filardo, Jesal Kapadia, Aglaya Oleynikova, Alessandra Pomarico, Teresa Roversi, Begonia Santa Cecilia and the Art Lab social center in Parma that generously hosted our workshop.

Thanks also to Jesse Jones, Tessa Giblin, Rachel Anderson, and Cis Boyle, for their friendship, their support and the time spent together discussing body politics and sculpting Sheelagh-na-gigs. Thank you, Jesse, for your powerful *Tremble,*

Tremble (2017), recasting the maternal body for a new political imagination.

Special thanks to Camille Barbagallo, who has edited this work, and to the publications where some of the articles included in the volume have previously appeared.

I also wish to acknowledge the contribution to my work of Feminist Research on Violence, the women's group in New York with whom I conspire to change the world and produce the website that carries this name (http://feministresearchonviolence.org). Thank you for the knowledge, affection, and enthusiasm we share at our meetings, which sustain and inspire my writing.

Finally, thanks to the editors of the books and journals in which some of the articles here collected were first published.

"With Philosophy and Terror: Transforming Bodies into Labor Power" was previously published in Athanasios Marvakis et al., eds., *Doing Psychology under New Conditions* (Concord, Ontario: Captus Press), 2–10.

"Mormons in Space Revisited" is a remake of an article published with George Caffentzis in *Midnight Notes* 2, no. 1 (1982): 3–12.

"In Praise of the Dancing Body" was previously published in Gods and Radicals, eds., *A Beautiful Resistance* no. 1 (August 22, 2016): 83–86.

"On Joyful Militancy" is an edited extract from an interview entitled "Feeling Powers Growing," published in *Joyful Militancy: Building Thriving Resistance in Toxic Times*, eds. Nick Montgomery and carla bergman (Chico, CA: AK Press, 2018).

Introduction

Beyond the Periphery of the Skin was originally devised as a response to the questions generated in the three lectures I gave at the California Institute of Integral Studies in the winter of 2015, on the meaning of the body and body politics in the feminist movement of the 1970s and in my own theoretical work. These lectures had multiple purposes: to stress the contribution that the feminism of the 1970s has given to a theory of the body, now greatly underestimated by new generations of feminists; to acknowledge, at the same time, its incapacity to devise strategies capable of significantly changing the material conditions of women's lives; and to present the framework that I developed in *Caliban and the Witch* to examine the roots of the forms of exploitation to which women have been subjected in the history of capitalist society.

In this sense, my presentation was a rethinking of the lessons learned from the past. Yet the discussions that followed the lectures raised questions that exceeded the original framework, convincing me to broaden the horizon of my lectures and of this book. Four questions stand out as essential to this current volume. First, is "women" still a necessary category for feminist politics, considering the diversities of histories and experiences covered under this label, or should we discard it, as Butler and other poststructuralist theorists have proposed that we do? More broadly, should we reject any political identity as inevitably fictitious and opt for unities built on purely oppositional grounds? How should we evaluate the new reproductive technologies that promise to restructure our physical makeup and remake our bodies in ways that better conform to our desires? Do these technologies enhance our control over our bodies or do they turn our bodies into objects of experimentation and profit-making at the service of the capitalist market and the medical profession?

With the exception of Part One, the book is organized around these questions, though Part One is a preparation for them, in that my implicit aim there is to demonstrate that the feminist movement of the 1970s must be evaluated primarily on the basis of the strategies it adopted, rather than its gendered standpoint. In this, the position I have defended differs significantly from that of "performance" theorists who have been more prone to criticize the 1970s women's liberation movement for its alleged identity politics than for the actual political strategies it has embraced.

Developed in the early 1990s—at a time when feminism was undergoing a major crisis due to the impact of an institutional takeover, the entrance of women into male-dominated occupations, and an economic restructuring that demanded a more gender-fluid workforce—poststructuralist theories postulating that bodies and genders are the products of discursive practices and performance were undoubtedly appealing, and to many they may continue to be. But it should be clear that if "women" is discarded as an analytic/political category, then "feminism" must follow suit, insofar as it is hard to imagine an oppositional movement emerging in the absence of a common experience of suffered injustice and abuse. Indeed, employers, as well as the courts, have been quick to take advantage of the feminist claim of an irreducible diversity among women, through the denial of a class certification status for women workers of companies (like Walmart) denouncing gender discrimination, and forcing them, instead, to file their complaints individually.[1] More importantly, surely can we conceive of experiences like maternity, childraising, and social subordination to men as constituting a *common terrain of struggle for women* even if it is one in which contrasting strategies may develop? Are alternative identities, such as gay, trans, and queer, less subject to fragmentation on the basis of class, race, ethnic origin, and age?

I write these words after watching the astounding images coming from the streets of Buenos Aires and other parts of Argentina, where for a number of years now women have poured by the hundreds of thousands to fight, despite their diversities and often disagreements—against violence against women, against women's indebtedness, and for the right to abortion, making collective decisions that transform what it means to be a woman. What would such struggles be without the recognition of "women" as a political subject, as an identity that is clearly contested but also constantly redefined in ways that are important for constructing a vision of the world we strive to create?

This is the argument that I have developed in the second part of the book, where I propose that denying the possibility of any social, political identification is a guide to defeat. It is a denial of solidarity among the living and with the dead, and truly imagining peoples without histories. A further sobering thought is that every general concept is constructed in the presence of great differences. We cannot more confidently speak of love, education, and death than we can of women, men, and trans, if we consider diversity a precluding element. We know, for instance, that love in ancient Greece and Rome was a widely different from love as experienced in the twentieth century in Europe or the US, or love experienced in a polygamous context. This does not prevent us from using the concept and many others similarly constructed, for short of that we would be reduced to silence.

Part Two also examines what can be defined as a new body-remake movement, in which both technological innovations and the medical profession play a major role. My goal in this case is more to highlight what is at stake and warn against the implicit dangers than to criticize the practices involved. Body remakes widely differ, ranging from plastic surgery to surrogacy and gender reassignment. But what looms large in each case is the power and prestige that medical experts have gained because of the life changes they promise. Such dependence on an institution that has a long history of cooperation with capital and the state should be a concern for us. History should be a guide in this context.

In Part Three, I have included articles discussing the role of medicine and psychology in the organization and disciplining of industrial workers as well as women as subjects of reproductive work. Part Three also looks back at the discussions, incipient in the Reagan era, of the kind of workforce needed for work in new technological environments and extraterrestrial sites. The capitalist dream, represented in "Mormons in Space," of an ascetic worker capable of overcoming the inertia of a body constructed over millions of years and functioning, for instance, in space colonies, is instructive today as capital development of artificial intelligence calls for new skills and a remodeling of subjectivities. At present, the concrete expression of such dream is the installation in our brains of microchips enabling those who can afford them to enhance their capacities and free themselves of passports and keys. But visions already abound of a time when select individuals for sure will operate as pure minds, able to store large amount of memory and think at a great velocity, reading, for instance, a book in half an hour. Meanwhile, experimentation with the dismembering and recombining of our bodies is also proceeding at an accelerating pace, pointing to a world in which cloning, gene editing, and gene transfers—already carried out with animals—will be part of the medical/scientific kit, presumably allowing a future capitalist world to produce not only inanimate commodities but new forms of human life.

In this context, reclaiming our body, reclaiming our capacity to decide about our corporeal reality, begins by affirming the power and wisdom of the body as we know it, in that it has formed over a long period of time, in constant interaction with the formation of the earth, in ways that are tampered with at great risk for our well-being. "In Praise of the Dancing Body," the article that stands as the conclusion of the book, which I wrote after watching a dance that choreographer Daria Fain produced on the rise of consciousness and language, celebrates this power and wisdom that capitalism today wants to destroy. My vision here differs from the Bakhtinian conception of the Pantagruelian body, as imagined by Rabelais in six-teenth-century France. This is a body that expands beyond the periphery of its skin, but by appropriating, ingesting all that is eatable in the world, in an orgy of sensual pleasure and liberation from all constraints. My conception is equally expansive but of a different nature. For what it finds, in going beyond the periphery of the skin, is not a culinary paradise but a magical continuity with the other living organisms that populate the earth: the bodies of humans and the not-humans, the trees, the rivers, the sea, the stars. This is the image of a body that reunites what capitalism has divided, a body no longer constituted as a Leibnizian monad, without windows and without doors, but moving instead in harmony with cosmos, in a world where diversity is a wealth for all and a ground of commoning rather than a source of divisions and antagonisms.

Notes

1   In 2013 the Supreme Court rejected the class action brought by female employees of Walmart denouncing discrimination with regard to payment and conditions of work, arguing that women do not constitute a class, by virtue of their diversity, and that Walmart employees should file their complaints individually.

PART ONE

ONE

Lecture One
The Body, Capitalism, and the Reproduction of Labor Power

There is no doubt that the body is today at the center of political, disciplinary, and scientific discourse, with the attempt in every field to redefine its main qualities and possibilities. It is the sphinx to be interrogated and acted upon on the path toward social and individual change. Nevertheless, it is nearly impossible to articulate a coherent view of the body on the basis of the theories most accredited in the intellectual and political arena. On the one hand, we have the most extreme forms of biological determinism, with the assumption of the DNA as the *deus absconditus* (hidden god) presumably determining, behind our backs, our physiological and psychological life. On the other, we have (feminist, trans) theories encouraging us to discard all "biological" factors in favor of performative or textual representations of the body and to embrace, as constitutive of our being, our growing assimilation with the world of machines.

A common trend, however, is the absence of a standpoint from which to identify the social forces that are affecting our bodies. With an almost religious obsession, biologists circumscribe the area of significant activity to a microscopic world of molecules, whose constitution is as mysterious as that of the original sin. As far as biologists are concerned, we come into this world already tainted by, predisposed to, predestined to, or spared from disease, for all is in the DNA an unknown god has allotted to us. As for the discursive/performative theories of the body, they too are silent concerning the social ground from which ideas about the body and body practices are generated. There is perhaps the fear that searching for a unitary cause may blind us to the diverse ways in which our bodies articulate our identities and relations to power. There is also a tendency, recuperated from Foucault, to investigate the "effects" of the powers acting on our bodies rather than their sources. Yet without a reconstruction of the field of forces in which they move, our bodies must remain unintelligible or elicit mystifying views of their operations. How, for instance, can we envisage "going beyond the binary" without an understanding of its economic, political, and social utility within particular systems of exploitation, and, on the other hand, an understanding of the struggles by which gender identities are continuously transformed? How to speak of our "performance" of gender, race, and age without a recognition of the compulsion generated by specific forms of exploitation and punishment?

We must identify the world of antagonistic policies and power relations by which our bodies are constituted and rethink the struggles that have taken place in opposition to the "norm" if we are to devise strategies for change.

This is the work I have undertaken in *Caliban and the Witch* (2004), where I have examined how the transition to capitalism changed the concept and treatment of "the body,"[1] arguing that one of capitalism's main projects has been the *transformation of our bodies into work-machines*. This means that the need to maximize the exploitation of living labor, also through the creation of differentiated forms of work and coercion, has been the factor that more than any other has shaped our bodies in capitalist society. This approach has consciously contrasted with Foucault's,[2] which roots the disciplinary regimes to which the body was subjected at the beginning of the "modern era" in the workings of a metaphysical "Power" not better identified in its purposes and objectives.[3]

In contrast to Foucault, I have also argued that we do not have one but multiple histories of the body, that is, multiple histories of how the mechanization of the body was articulated, for the racial, sexual, and generational hierarchies that capitalism has constructed from its inception rule out the possibility of a universal standpoint. Thus the history of "the body" must be told by weaving together the histories of those who were enslaved, colonized, or turned into waged workers or unpaid housewives and the histories of the children, keeping in mind that these classifications are not mutually exclusive and that our subjection to "interlocking systems of domination" always produces a new reality.[4] I would add that we also need a history of capitalism written from the viewpoint of the animal world and of course the lands, the seas, and the forests.

We need to look at "the body" from all these viewpoints to grasp the depth of the war that capitalism has waged against human beings and "nature" and to devise strategies capable of ending such destruction. To speak of a war is not to assume an original wholeness or propose an idealized view of "nature." It is to highlight the state of emergency in which we currently live and to question, in an age that promotes remaking our bodies as a path to social empowerment and self-determination, the benefits that we may derive from policies and technologies that are not controlled from below. Indeed, before we celebrate our becoming cyborgs, we should reflect on the social consequences of the mechanization process that we have already undergone.[5] It is naive, in fact, to imagine that our symbiosis with machines necessarily results in an extension of our powers and ignore the constraints that technologies place on our lives and their increasing use as a means of social control as well as the ecological cost of their production.[6]

Capitalism has treated our bodies as work-machines because it is the social system that most systematically has made of human labor the essence of the accumulation of wealth and has most needed to maximize its exploitation. It has accomplished this in different ways: with the imposition of more intense and uniform forms of labor as well as multiple disciplinary regimes and institutions and with terror and rituals of degradation. Exemplary were those that in the seventeenth century were imposed on the inmates of the Dutch workhouses, who were forced to pulverize blocks of wood with the most backward and backbreaking method, for no useful purpose but to be taught to obey external orders and to experience in every fiber of their bodies their impotence and subjection.[7]

Another example of the debasement rituals employed to break people's will to resistance were those imposed, since the turn of the twentieth century, by doctors in South Africa, on Africans destined to work in the gold mines (Butchart 1998, 92–110). Under the guise of "heat tolerance tests" or "selection procedures," African workers were ordered to strip naked, line up, and shovel rocks and then submit to radiographic examinations or to measurements by tape and weighing scales, all under the gaze of medical examiners, who often remained invisible to those thus tested (94, 97, 100). The goal of the exercise was supposedly to demonstrate to future workers the sovereign power of the mining industry and to initiate Africans to a life in which they would be "deprived of any human dignity" (94).

In the same time period, in Europe and the US, Taylorism's time and motion studies—later incorporated into the construction of the assembly line—turned the mechanization of the workers' bodies into a scientific project, through the fragmentation and atomization of tasks, the elimination of any decisional element from the work process, and, above all, the stripping of the work itself from any knowledge and motivational factor.[8] Automatism, however, has also been the product of a work life of infinite repetition, a life of "No Exit,"[9] like the nine-to-five in a factory or office, where even the holiday breaks become mechanized and routine, due to their time constraints and predictability.

Foucault was right, however: the "repressive hypothesis" is not sufficient to explain the history of the body in capitalism.[10] As important as what was repressed have been the "capacities" that were developed. In *Principles of Economics* (1890), the British economist Alfred Marshall celebrated the capacities that capitalist discipline has produced in the industrial workforce, declaring that few populations in the world were capable of what European workers at the time could do. He praised industrial workers' "general ability" to keep working continuously, for hours, on the same task, to remember everything, to remember, while doing a task, what the next one should be, to work with instruments without breaking them, without wasting time, to be careful in handling expensive machinery and steady even doing the most monotonous tasks. These, he argued, were unique skills that few people worldwide possessed, demonstrating, in his view, that even work that appears unskilled is actually highly skilled (Marshall [1890] 1990, 172).

Marshall would not say how such wonderful, machinelike workers were created. He did not say that people had to be separated from the land and terrorized with exemplary tortures and executions. Vagabonds had their ears cut. Prostitutes were subjected to "waterboarding," the same type of torture to which the CIA and US Special Forces subject those they accuse of "terrorism." Tied to a chair, women suspected of improper behavior were plunged into ponds and rivers to the point of near suffocation. Slaves were whipped until the flesh was torn from their bones and were burned, mutilated, left under a blazing sun until their bodies putrefied.

As I have argued in *Caliban and the Witch*, with the development of capitalism not only were communal fields "enclosed," so was the body. But this process has differed for men and women, in the same way as it has differed for those who were destined to be enslaved and those who were subjected to other forms of coerced labor, waged work included.

Women, in capitalist development, have suffered a double process of mechanization. Besides being subjected to the discipline of work, paid and unpaid, in plantations, factories, and homes, they have been expropriated from their bodies and turned into sexual objects and breeding machines.

Capitalist accumulation (as Marx recognized) is the accumulation of workers.[11] This was the motivation driving the slave trade, the development of the plantation system and—I have argued—the witch hunts that took place in Europe and the "New World."[12] Through the persecution of "witches," women wishing to control their reproductive capacity were denounced as enemies of children and, in different ways, subjected to a demonization that has continued into the present. In the nineteenth century, for instance, advocates of "free love," like Victoria Woodhull, were branded in the American press as satanic, pictured with devil's wings and all (Poole 2009). Today as well, in several US states, women who go to a clinic to abort have to make their ways through masses of "right-to-lifers" screaming "baby killers" and chasing them, thanks to a ruling by the Supreme Court,[13] as far as the clinic's door.

In no place has the attempt to reduce women's bodies to machines been more systematic, brutal and normalized than in slavery. While exposed to constant sexual assaults and the searing pain of seeing their children sold as slaves, after England banned the slave trade in 1807, enslaved women in the US were forced to procreate to fuel a breeding industry with its center in Virginia.[14] "As the power looms of Lancashire sucked up all the cotton that the South could grow," Ned and Constance Sublette have written, "women's wombs "were not merely the source of local enrichment, but were also suppliers in a global system of agricultural input, enslaved industrial input, and financial expansion" (Sublette and Sublette 2016, 414). Thomas Jefferson approved, going to great lengths to have the US Congress limit the importation of slaves from Africa in order to protect the prices of the slaves that women on the Virginian plantations would procreate. "I consider," he wrote, "a woman who brings a child every two years more profitable than the best man on the farm. What she produces is an addition to the capital, while his labors disappear in mere consumption" (416).

Although in the history of the US no group of women, outside of slavery, has been directly compelled to have children, with the criminalization of abortion, involuntary procreation and state control of the female body have been institutionalized. The advent of the birth control pill has not decisively altered this situation. Even in countries where abortion has been legalized, restrictions have been introduced that make access difficult for many women.[15] This is because procreation has an economic value that in no way is diminished on account of capital's increased technological power. It is a mistake, in fact, to assume that the interest of the capitalist class in the control over women's reproductive capacity may be diminishing on account of its ability to replace workers with machines. Despite its tendency to make workers redundant and create "surplus populations," capital accumulation still requires human labor. Only labor creates value, machines do not. The very growth of technological production, as Danna (2019, 208ff) has recently argued, is made possible by the existence of social inequalities and the intense exploitation of workers in the "Third World." What is vanishing today is the compensation for work that in the past was waged, not the work itself. Capitalism needs workers, it also needs consumers and soldiers. Thus, the actual size of the population is still a matter of great political importance. This is why—as Jenny Brown has shown in her *Birth Strike* (2018)—restrictions are placed on abortion. So important is for the capitalist class to control women's bodies that, as we have seen, even in the US, where in the 1970s abortion was legalized, attempts to reverse this decision continue to this day. In other countries, Italy for instance, the loophole is conceding to doctors the possibility of becoming "conscientious objectors," with the result that many women cannot abort in the localities where they live.

However, control over women's bodies has never been a purely quantitative matter. Always, state and capital have tried to determine who is allowed to reproduce and who is not. This is why we simultaneously have restrictions on the right to abort and the criminalization of pregnancy,[16] in the case of women who are expected to generate "troublemakers." It is no accident, for instance, if from the 1970s to the 1990s, as new generations of Africans, Indians, and other decolonized subjects were coming to political age, demanding a restitution of the wealth that Europeans had robbed from their countries, a massive campaign to contain what was defined as a "population explosion" was mounted throughout the former colonial world (Hartmann 1995, 189–91), with the promotion of sterilization and contraceptives, like Depo Provera, Norplant, IUDs that, once implanted, women could not control.[17] Through the sterilization of women in the former colonial world, international capital has attempted to contain a worldwide struggle for reparations; in the same way that, in the US, successive governments have tried to block black people's liberation struggle through the mass incarceration of millions of young black men and women.

Like every other form of reproduction, procreation too has a clear class character and is racialized. Relatively few women worldwide can today decide whether to have children and the conditions in which to have them. As Dorothy Roberts has so powerfully shown in *Killing the Black Body* ([1997] 2017), while white, affluent women's desire to procreate is now elevated to the rank of an unconditional right, to be guaranteed at all costs, black women, for whom it is more difficult to have some economic security, are ostracized and penalized if they have a child. Yet the discrimination that so many black, migrant, proletarian women encounter on the way to maternity should not be read as a sign that capitalism is no longer interested in demographic growth. As I previously argued, capitalism cannot dispense with workers. The workerless factory is an ideological sham intended to scare workers into subjection. Were labor to be eliminated from the production process capitalism would probably collapse. Population expansion is by itself a stimulus to growth; thus, no sector of capital can be indifferent to whether women decide to procreate.

This point is forcibly made by the already-quoted *Birth Strike*, where Jenny Brown thoroughly analyses the relation of procreation to every aspect of economic and social life, convincingly demonstrating that politicians today are concerned about the worldwide decline of the birth rate, which she reads as a silent strike. Brown suggests that women should consciously take advantage of this concern to bargain better conditions of living and work. In other words, she suggests that we use our capacity to reproduce *as a tool of political power*.[18] This is a tempting proposition. It is tempting to imagine women openly going on a birth strike, declaring, for instance, that "we won't bring any more children into this world until the conditions that await them are drastically changed." I say "openly" because, as Brown documents it, a broad-based though silent refusal of procreation is already taking place. The worldwide decline of the birth rate, that has peaked in countries like Italy and Germany since the post–World War II period, has been the sign of such a reproduction strike. The birth rate has been declining for some time in the US as well. Women today have fewer children because it means less housework, less dependence on men or a job, because they refuse to see their lives consumed by maternal duties, or have no desire to reproduce themselves and, especially in the US, because they have no access to contraceptive and abortion.[19] It is hard, however, to see how an open strike could be organized. Many of the children born are not planned or wanted. Moreover, in many countries, having a child is for women an insurance policy toward the future. In countries where there is no social security or pension system, having a child may be the only possibility of survival and the only way that a woman can have access to land or can gain social recognition. Children can also be a source of joy, often the only wealth a woman has. Our task, then, is not to tell women that they should not have children, but to make sure that women can decide whether to have them and to ensure that mothering is not costing us our lives.

The social power that mothering potentially gives women is plausibly the reason why under the guise of fighting infertility and giving women more options, doctors are striving to reproduce life outside the uterus. This is no easy task. Despite much talk of "test-tube babies," "ectogenesis" remains a medical utopia. But in vitro fertilization (IVF), genetic screening, and other reproductive technologies are paving the way to the creation of artificial wombs. Some feminists may approve. In the 1970s feminists like Shulamith Firestone hailed the day when women would be liberated from procreation, which she considered the cause of a history of oppression.[20] But this is a dangerous stand. If capitalism is an unjust, exploitative social system, it is worrisome to think that in the future capitalist planners might be able to produce the kind of human beings that they need. We should not underestimate this danger. Even without gene editing we are already mutants, capable, for instance, of carrying out our daily lives while aware that catastrophic events are occurring all around us, including the destruction of our ecological environment and the slow death of the many people now living on our streets, whom we daily pass by without much of a thought or an emotion. What threatens us are not only that the machines are taking over, but also that we are becoming like machines. Thus, we do not need any more robot-like individuals produced by a new breeding industry, this time located in medical labs.

As the generation of feminists to which I belong has struggled to establish, maternity is not a destiny. But it is also not something to be programmatically avoided, as if it were the cause of women's misery and exploitation. No more than possessing a uterus or a breast is the capacity to give birth a curse—one from which a medical profession (that has sterilized us, lobotomized us, ridiculed us when we cried in pain giving birth) must liberate us. Nor is maternity a gender-performing act. Rather it should be understood as a political, value-positing decision. In a self-governing, autonomous society such decisions would be taken in consideration of our collective well-being, the available resources, and the preservation of the natural wealth. Today as well, such considerations cannot be ignored, but the decision to have a child must also be seen as a refusal to allow capital's planners to decide who is allowed to live and who instead must die or cannot even be born.

Notes

1   I place the "the body" in quotation marks to indicate the fictional character of the concept, as an abstraction from different, unique social histories and realities.

2   See Foucault's *Discipline and Punish: The Birth of the Prison* (1979).

3   It is worth mentioning here the critique of Foucault's analysis of the "political economy of the body" made by Dario Melossi in *The Prison and the Factory* (1981), 44–45. He writes:

> This bourgeois *construction* of the body in the school, the barracks, the prison and the family remains completely incomprehensible . . . unless we start from the capitalistic management of the labour process (and *at this moment* in the history of capitalism). This had to set itself the task of structuring the body as a machine inside the productive machine as a whole, that is, we must understand that the organisation of work does not treat the body as something extraneous, it *steps through* the body into the muscles and into the head, reorganising simultaneously with the productive process that fundamental part of itself constituted by the labour-power of the body. In sum, in this age the *machine* constitutes a compound invention in which there resides a dead, inorganic, fixed element and a live, organic variable one. (italics in original)

4   I take the concept of interlocking systems of domination—central to intersectionality theory—from bell hooks (1990), 59. Also hooks (1989), 175.

5   My reference here is to Donna Haraway's "Cyborg Manifesto" (1991), which I find theoretically and politically very problematic.

6   On the carceral and surveillance use of technology, see R. Benjamin ed., *Captivating Technologies* (2019).

7   See Melossi and Pavarini (1981).

8   On this topic see H. Braverman (1974), above all chap. 4, "Scientific Management," and chap. 5, "The Scientific-Technical Revolution and the Worker."

9   The reference is to the 1944 play by Jean-Paul Sartre, in which hell is described as the self-imprisonment to which we are condemned when we cannot free ourselves from the constraints placed on our lives by our past actions.

10 By the "repressive hypothesis" Foucault refers to the tendency among historians to describe the effects of capitalism on social life and discipline only in terms of repression. He has argued, instead, that a major development in the capitalist treatment of sexuality has been a "veritable discursive explosion" about sex, indeed the transformation of sex into discourse, by means of which "legal sanctions against minor perversions were multiplied." *The History of Sexuality*, vol. 1, 17, 36–37. While I consider Foucault's emphasis on the "discursive turn," by means of which sex was transformed into an immaterial good, brilliant but reductive, I agree with his insistence on the productive character of social discipline and even social repression. Psychic dynamism seems to be governed by a law similar to that of the conservation of energy, whereby the prohibition of particular forms of behavior does not produce a vacuum, but substitutive, compensatory responses of which the translation of repressed desire into "discourse" is one.

11 See, e.g., *Capital*, vol. 1, pt. 7, chap. 25, p. 764: "The reproduction of labour-power which must incessantly be re-incorporated into capital as its means of valorization . . . forms in fact a factor in the reproduction of capital itself. *Accumulation of capital is therefore the multiplication of the proletariat*. (italics mine)

12 Federici (2004), especially chap. 4.

13 In June 2014, the Supreme Court unanimously struck down a Massachusetts law forbidding protesters from standing within thirty-five feet of the entrance to a reproductive health care facility. As a consequence of this decision, now women who go to a clinic for an abortion must be escorted, as protesters have the right to follow them up to the entrance door, creating an extremely tense and threatening situation.

14 See Sublette and Sublette (2016) and Beckles (1989), especially chap. 5, "Breeding Wenches and Labor Supply Policies." While in the US the center of the slave breeding industry was Virginia, in the Caribbean

Islands it was Barbados, "the only sugar plantation colony that by 1807 succeeded in eliminating an economic need for African slave imports as a result of a positive natural growth in the slave stock" (Beckles 1989, 91). Beckles adds that by the eighteenth century, slave "breeding" "emerged as a popular policy, and the term became commonplace in managerial language concerning labor supply" (92).

15   In the US restrictions have been introduced over the years, in several states, that reduce the time period in which abortions can be allowed and make the procedure conditional on parental consent. There is currently a drive to ban abortion altogether. The measure passed on May 14, 2019, by the Alabama Senate that prohibits abortion at every stage is but one example.

16   This is the term Lynn Paltrow, the founder and executive director of National Advocates for Pregnant Women, and Jeanne Flavin have used, in a 2013 study, to describe policies introduced in the US to regulate pregnancy, which affect especially indigent black women (Paltrow and Flavin 2013, 299–343). Such is the present legal situation—they wrote—that by deciding to have a child, poor black women place themselves outside the boundary of the constitution, becoming vulnerable to charges that would never be consider crimes under different circumstances. Women, for instance, have been arrested and jailed for being in a car accident when pregnant and for using legal drugs possibly affecting the fetuses. A turning point in this process has been the conviction for homicide and child abuse, by the South Carolina Supreme Court, in 2003, of a woman who had a still birth, presumably after having used drugs during her pregnancy. Following that decision, scores of women have been charged with child abuse for having used illegal drugs while pregnant, as fetuses in several have been legally defined as persons. On this subject, see also the website Feminist Research on Violence / Plataforma Feminista sobre Violencias https://feministresearchonviolence.org.

17   See again on this subject Hartmann (1995) especially chap. 3, "Contraceptive Controversies," and Connelly (2008).

18   Jenny Brown (2018), 153, and on the same subject see chap. 11: "Controlling the Means of Reproduction" (143–60).

19   Jenny Brown (2018), 144. Brown argues that difficult access to birth control and abortion is the true reason for the fact that until recently women in the United States had a higher fertility rate, adding that, in 2011, 45 percent of birth in the United States were unplanned, in the sense of unwanted or mistimed.

20   In *The Dialectic of Sex* (1970), Firestone advocated the "freeing of women from the tyranny of their reproductive biology by every means," as a project however to be realized in a postrevolutionary society. (206) For a discussion of "Feminist Concerns about

Ectogenesis," see Murphy (1995), 113–33. Murphy argues that ectogenesis is the medical practice that poses the most direct threat to women's reproductive rights and most devalue women's contribution to reproduction. She also mentions the fear that the construction of artificial wombs could lead to "femicides" (125).

TWO

Lecture Two
"Body Politics" in the
Feminist Revolt

In my previous essay, I have argued that capitalism, as a system based on the exploitation of human labor, has defined women as bodies—that is, as beings dominated by their biology, insofar as it has appropriated our reproductive capacity and put it at the service of the reproduction of the workforce and the labor market. This is not to say that in the history of capitalism women have not been subjected to other forms of exploitation. Enslaved women in the American plantations have worked in the fields, cut canes, and picked cotton. Under the Jim Crow system, black women built roads as part of chain gangs. In Britain, France, and the US, working-class women and children were the backbone of the industrial revolution and, even after they were excluded from the factories, they always integrated the family budget with some part-time work. This has been particularly true in the case of black women who could never rely on a steady male wage. The point, however, is that regardless of what other labors we had to perform, *procreation and sexual service to men have always been expected of us and often forced upon us.* While legally denied the possibility of maternity, under slavery black women raised the children of their masters, suffered their sexual assaults, and were forced to procreate for the slave-breeding industry that developed especially after the abolition of the slave trade in 1806.

Women have always fought against this appropriation of our bodies and the violence that has come with it. Enslaved women used their knowledge of contraceptive herbs to prevent conception and even killed their children at birth to ensure that they would not be enslaved. At the risk of losing their lives and suffering terrible tortures they resisted their masters' sexual assaults. As Dorothy Roberts ([1997] 2017, 45) writes: "They escaped from the plantations, feigned illness, endured severe punishments. . . . A common recollection of former slaves was the sight of a woman . . . being beaten for defying her master's sexual advances. . . . No doubt there were, as well, many cases of slave women poisoning their masters in retaliation for sexual molestation."

Nothing—short of incarceration—can match the violence of enslavement. Yet the word comes to mind when we think of the desperation that many women have felt when discovering being pregnant against their will, which often cost their lives. *Women's struggle to avoid pregnancy and to avoid sex, inside and outside of marriage, is one of the most common and unrecognized on earth.* But it was not until the 1970s that feminists began to organize, openly and on a mass level, to fight under the banner of "body politics" for control over our sexuality and for the right to decide whether to procreate. Body politics expressed the realization that our most intimate, presumably "private" experiences are in reality highly political matters of great of concern to the nation-state, as demonstrated by the extensive legislation that governments have historically adopted to regulate them. Body politics also recognized that our capacity to produce new lives has subjected us to forms of exploitation far more extensive, invasive, and degrading than those that men have suffered, and more difficult to resist. While men have confronted capitalist exploitation collectively and "on the job," women have confronted it individually, in their relations with men, in the home, in hospitals while giving birth, in the streets, and as target of abusive comments and assaults.

Feminism was a revolt against our being defined as "bodies," only valued for our imagined readiness for self-sacrifice and servicing other people. It was a revolt against the assumption that the best that we can expect from life is to be the domestic and sexual servants of men and the producers of workers and soldiers for the state. By fighting for the right to abortion and against the barbarous ways in which most of us are forced to give birth, against rape in and out of the family, against sexual objectification and the myth of the vaginal orgasm, we began to unravel the ways in which our bodies have been shaped by the capitalist division of labor.[1]

Much of the feminist movement's politics centered on the struggle for abortion, but the revolt against the prescribed feminine norm was more profound. Not only the duty to become mothers but the very conception of "femininity" was questioned and rejected. *It was the feminist movement that denaturalized femininity.* The critique of the normative construction of womanhood began long before Judith Butler argued that gender is a "performance." The critique of heteronormativity, of the sexual binary and "womanhood" as a biological concept and, above all, the rejection of "biology as destiny" predate by many years *Gender Trouble* (1990) and Butler's subsequent theoretical production as well as the development of the queer, intersex, and trans rights movements. Feminists did not only write about the end of "womanhood," they acted to bring it about. Symbolically, on the first day of the opening of Congress, in Washington, DC, on January 15, 1968, radical feminists led by Shulamith Firestone organized a torchlit funeral procession, calling it the "The Burial of Traditional Womanhood," "who passed," as the flyer read, "after 3000 years of bolstering the egos of warmakers and aiding the cause of war."[2] They also protested bridal fairs, denounced the duty and compulsion to be "beautiful," called themselves "witches."

Feminists rejected the repressive sexuality that passed as sexual liberation. They also "sparked off a self-help movement that by 1975 had built thirty women-controlled clinics across the United States, educating women about their bodies and placing health as a central issue in feminist politics at home and abroad. It is thanks to this movement that thousands of women began to practice 'self-examination.'"[3] In this way, the women's liberation movement helped us to overcome the shame that we had always felt about our bodies, especially our genital organs, and taught us to discuss issues, like menstruation and menopause previously considered taboo. It was through the feminist movement that many women of the postwar generation were exposed to "sexual education" and came to understand the political implications of sexuality in all its dimensions. Our interactions with men were also put under scrutiny, revealing their violence as well as men's insistence on infantilizing and degrading us—calling us "baby," "chicks," "broads," and expecting sexual quid pro quos for every favor, like paying for our dinner on a date.

The demand for safe contraceptives and the possibility to refuse unwanted pregnancies was our declaration of independence from men and from the state and capital, which for centuries have terrorized us with punitive laws and practices. Our struggle, however, has shown that we cannot reclaim our bodies without changing the material conditions of our lives. The limit of the struggle for abortion was that it did not seek to enable all women to have the children we wanted. This was a political mistake, as so many women, in the United States, have been denied the right to be mothers, during slavery by the law and subsequently through lack of resources and forced sterilizations. Thousands of black women and men in the US were sterilized in the 1920s and 1930s, and for many more years afterward, as part of a eugenics campaign aimed to prevent the reproduction of "feebleminded races," a category that also included many immigrant people.

Working-class white women were also sterilized, during the Depression, when they were considered "feebleminded," the category that social workers and doctors used to label women deemed promiscuous and likely to have children out of marriage (Le Sueur 1984). In the 1930s, authorities, across the US, welcomed the eugenic programs that the Nazis were carrying out. US government officials saw Nazi Germany as the fulfillment of their own eugenic plans, praising sterilization as the road to a better society. Crucially, the support for such programs would have continued except that, after the US entered World War II, Nazism became discredited (Nourse 2008, 127–33). But though the government's plan to sterilize all "unfit" people was officially brought to an end for men in 1947, sterilization for women has continued. As recently as the 1960s and even the 1970s, many women on welfare were forced to accept sterilization if they wished to continue to receive their payments. The documentary *No Más Bebés* (Tajima-Pena 2015) documented the plight of hundreds of immigrant women who, in the 1960s and early 1970s, were sterilized at a University of Southern California medical center in Los Angeles County without their consent, many not discovering what had happened to them until years later when they realized they could not become pregnant again.

It was a mistake, then, for the feminist movement not to connect the struggle for abortion to the struggle to change the material conditions of women's lives and (for instance) not mobilize against the political attack that in the late '60s the government moved against Aid to Families with Dependent Children, the welfare program that since the 1930s had enabled women without a job and a husband to have money of their own from the state. The absence of the feminist movement from the welfare struggle was especially problematic because in the official discourse welfare was always racialized, even though the majority of women on the rolls were white women. Black women, however, were more visible because they were more combative and organized, drawing strength from the legacy of the civil rights and Black Power movements. It was black women who led the struggle to expand the resources that the welfare program provided and to change its public image. But their message that "every mother is a working woman" and that raising children is a service to society should have spoken to all women.[4]

The welfare mothers' struggle, however, never gained the support it would have needed to prevent the state from waging a vicious war on the program and the women themselves, a war that had disastrous consequences for the black community. For as Dorothy Roberts ([1997] 2017, 202–22) writes, it was the war on welfare that created the image of the black single mother, "parasitically" depending on welfare, hooked on crack, and producing dysfunctional families, which served to justify the politics of mass incarceration.

The inability of the feminist movement to fight to guarantee that no woman should be denied the right to have children because of the material conditions of her life and the feminist representation of abortion as "choice" have created divisions between white and black women that we must not reproduce. It is one reason why many women of color have distanced themselves from feminism and organized a movement for reproductive justice that stresses precisely the need to connect the struggle over procreation with the one for economic justice.[5]

We see a similar dynamic emerging in the #metoo movement, as again many women fail to recognize that sexual violence is a structural problem and not an abuse of power by perverse men. To say that it is a structural problem means that women *are set up to be sexually abused by the economic conditions in which the majority of us are forced to live*. Clearly, if women earned higher wages, if waitresses did not depend on tips to pay the rent, if film directors and producers couldn't decide the future of young women who turn to them for jobs, if we could leave abusive relationships or jobs in which we are sexually harassed—then we would see a change. But this is not the reality for most women. It is also true that women stay in abusive situations, even if they are not economically dependent, because we are used to valuing ourselves depending on whether we please men. We have not been trained to value ourselves on the basis of what we do, of our accomplishments. This is part of a long process of conditioning that has not yet lost its grip on us. The feminist movement has been a turning point. It has changed and valorized what it means to be a woman. But that valorization has not translated into economic security. On the contrary, our poverty has grown along with our autonomy, which is why we see today women working at two or three jobs and even working as surrogate mothers.

In this context, the campaign that some feminists have undertaken to ban prostitution, as a uniquely degrading, violent activity, is self-defeating. Singling out sex work as especially degrading contributes to devaluing and blaming the women who practice it, without at the same time providing any clue about what options women really have. It obscures the fact that, in the absence of adequate means of subsistence, women have always had to sell their bodies and not only in brothels and the streets. We have sold our bodies in marriage. We have sold ourselves on the job—whether it was to keep a job, to gain one, to obtain a promotion or not be harassed by a supervisor. We have sold ourselves in universities and other cultural institutions and, as we have seen, in the movie industry. Women have also engaged in prostitution in support of their husbands. For years, in West Virginia, in the coal-mining areas, an informal system of prostitution existed whereby wives paid with their bodies for any problem their husbands had with the company, to ensure that they would not be laid off, to keep feeding their children when their husbands got sick and could no longer mine coal, or to maintain credit at the company store when the family's debts accumulated. In all these cases, a wife would be invited to a room upstairs to try on shoes displayed in the shoe department, where a cot was provided. Older women would warn the newcomers not to go upstairs, but need always prevailed.[6]

We should also acknowledge that there are ways of earning an income that are more degrading than prostitution. Selling our brains may be more dangerous and degrading than selling access to our vaginas. Calling for the criminalization of prostitution or more severe punishments for the clients further victimizes the most vulnerable in our communities and gives local immigration authorities a justification for deporting immigrants. This is not to say that we should not fight to improve the conditions of sex work and, above all, struggle to build a society where we do not have to sell our bodies. All over the world, sex workers are fighting for that.[7] Furthermore, as women gain more social power, the experience of being a sex worker and the conditions of sex work are changing. Sex workers are not just playthings in male hands, victims of their sadistic desires, controlled by pimps robbing them of their earnings. Many are women who use the money from sex work to pay for children's schooling, live and organize with other women, form cooperatives, set work conditions and prices, and provide each other with safety and protection. Sex work is a means of rounding up wages, paying for educational or health costs. For many women it is a part-time complement to housework or waged work. Interactive sex, performed through the internet as "webcamming," can be inserted in the interstices of domestic work. To be sure, *let's be abolitionists, but not only with respect to sex work. All forms of exploitation should be abolished, not just sex work.* Again, our task as feminists is not to tell other women what forms of exploitation are acceptable, but to expand our possibilities, so that we will not be compelled to sell ourselves in any way. We do so by reclaiming the means of our reproduction—the lands, the waters, the production of goods and knowledge, and our decision-making power, our capacity to decide what kind of lives we want and what kind of human beings we want to be.

This also applies to the question of gender identity. We cannot change our social identity without a struggle to change the economic/social conditions of our existence. Social identities are neither essences, fixed, frozen, determined once for all, nor groundless, infinitely shifting realities. And they are not defined purely by the norms that the capitalist system imposes on us. Social identities, including gender identities, are shaped by class, gender relations, and the struggles of the communities we come from. What being "woman" means to me, for instance, is very different from what it meant to my mother, because so many of us have fought to change our relation to marriage, to work, and to men.[8]

We must reject the idea that our social identities are completely defined by the capitalist system. The history of the feminist movement is exemplary in this context. Feminism has been a long battle against the norms, rules, and behavioral codes that have been imposed on us, which has significantly changed over time what it means to be a woman. As I have already stressed, feminists were the first to subvert the myth of an eternal, natural "femininity." Women's liberation was a commitment to create a more open-ended and fluid identity for women, one that would be constantly open to redefinition and reconstructions. The trans movement continues a process that has been underway since the 1970s and even earlier. What Butler has popularized is not new. Marxism and most twentieth-century philosophies—especially existentialism, an influence on Butler—have attacked the idea of a fixed, essential subject. Our bodies are shaped by class relations, as well as ethnic factors and the decisions we make in our lives.

Thus, the struggle to destabilize our assigned identities cannot be separated from the struggle to change the social/historical conditions of our lives and above all undermine social hierarchies and inequalities. I hope the trans and intersex movements learn from the lessons and the mistakes of the past—to grasp that we cannot fight for self-determination without changing how we work, how the wealth that we produce is used, and what access we have to it. These objectives cannot be achieved only by changing our names or bodily appearance. They require that we unite with other people to reclaim our collective power, to decide how we want to live, what kind of health and education we need to have, what kind of society we want to create.

It is also important to stress that we already live in a transitional world in which meanings and definitions are in flux, ambiguous, and contested. None is more ambiguous than "woman," an identity that is at the center of multiple assaults carrying opposite normative prescriptions. While an unequal sexual division of labor persists, women's entrance in once-masculine occupations and the increasing technologization of work have required an underdevelopment of feminine traits, a flight, so to speak, from the female body, also visible in the new models of female aesthetics, that emphasize a boyish look, the opposite of the all-curves body that until the 1960s was the pinnacle of male desire.[9] Already, in many occupations, conformity to a "feminine" gender model amounts to a self-devaluation, as—from academia to the art gallery and the computer lab—capitalism needs a genderless workforce.[10] This is not a universal rule. But what is certain is that the areas of work where the model of femininity celebrated (for instance) in the 1950s is still in demand are rapidly disappearing. From the viewpoint of work, we are already living in a gender-fluid world, in which we are expected to be feminine and masculine at the same time. Certainly, marriage, motherhood, and housework—once the identifying practices—are not enough, even from capital's viewpoint. We are expected to be independent, efficient, and work outside the home. More and more we are expected to be like men.

At the same time, women's presence in almost every aspect of social and political life is having an impact on the public image of work, and institutional decision making. It serves to eroticize work, it creates the illusion that what we do is useful, constructive. It humanizes policies otherwise very destructive. Even the organization of war appears more benign when the head of the military is a woman, as is the case currently in Germany. As women, we are particularly vulnerable to this manipulation, since we are not used to being appreciated and to seeing our work acknowledged and rewarded. In sum, both the identities of workers and women, as social/political subjects, are undergoing a significant change that we must take into account when discussing "identity politics." In the hands of government and other institutions, "identity politics" is a problem because it separates us into different groups, each with a set of rights—women's rights, gay rights, indigenous peoples' rights, trans rights—without acknowledging what stands in the way of our being treated with justice. We must be critical of any concept of identity that is not historical and transformative, that does not allow us to see our different and common forms of exploitation. But we need to address differently social identities that are rooted in particular forms of exploitation and are reshaped by a history of struggle still continuing in our time, for tracing our identities back to a history of exploitation and struggle allows us to find a common ground and collectively shape a more equitable vision of the future.

Notes

1   On the meaning and significance of "body politics," see Robin Morgan, ed., *Sisterhood Is Powerful* (1970) and Cherríe Moraga and Gloria Anzaldúa, eds., *This Bridge Called My Back* (1981).

2   For the oration at the event, read by Kathie Amatniek, see Chicago Women's Liberation Union Herstory Project, "Funeral Oration for the Burial of Traditional Womanhood," https://www.cwluherstory. org/classic-feminist-writings-articles/funeral-oration-for-the-burial-of-traditional-womanhood. A fuller account of the event is found in the Herstory Project from the Women's Studies Resources, Duke Special Collections Library https://repository.duke.edu/dc/wlmpc.

3   I quote from a letter sent to me, on January 21, 2015, by Carol Downer, one of the main founders of the self-help movement, to correct my criticism of the politics of the feminist movement with regard to the struggle for abortion. Downer reminded me that in the 1970s feminism was not a single-issue movement. Only in the late 1970s, with the development of the "pro-choice" strategy, did its horizon narrow to concentrate on upholding the right to abort. On this subject, see also the Boston Women's Health Book Collective, *Our Bodies, Ourselves: A Book by and for Women* (1976).

4   On the struggle of women on welfare and the institutional and media campaign against them see Milwaukee County Welfare Rights Center, *Welfare Mothers Speak Out* (1972) and Ellen Reese, *Backlash against Welfare Mothers* (2005).

5   As described in the website of SisterSong (https://www.sistersong. net/reproductive-justice), the reproductive justice movement was born in 1994, when in preparation for the International Conference on Population and Development to be held in Cairo that year, a group of black women gathering in Chicago decided that the women's rights movement could not represent the interests of women of color and other marginalized people.

6   See Michael Kline and Carrie Kline, "Esau in the Coalfields: Owing Our Souls to the Company Store," and Michael Kline, "Behind the Coal Curtain: Efforts to Publish the Esau Story in West Virginia" and "The Rented Girl: A Closer Look at Women in the Coalfields," in Harris (2017, 5–25, 27–30, 38–45).

7   On this subject, see Mac and Smith (2018). As they write in their opening pages: "Sex workers are everywhere. We are your neighbours. We brush past you on the street. Our kids go to the same school as yours . . ." "This book," they say, "is not about enjoying sex work. [It] will not argue that sex work is 'empowerment.' . . . "We are not interested in forming a movement with men who buy sex." "Our concern is for the safety and the survival of people who sell sex" (2–3).

8   On the question of "identity" and identity politics, see bell hooks: "The Politics of Radical Black Subjectivity" and "Postmodern Blackness." In *Yearning* (1990) 15–32. "There is a radical difference," she writes "between a repudiation of the idea that there is a black 'essence' and recognition of the way black identity has been specifically constituted in the experience of exile and struggle" (29).

9   For a powerful analysis of the new models of feminine beauty, see Bordo's *Unbearable Weight* (1993).

10 In *Mothernism* (2014, 142–43), the Danish artist Lise Haller Baggesen speaks of "coming out" as a mother, of refusing (as she put it) to "check motherhood at the door," in an art world where the mother is viewed as persona non grata.

THREE

Lecture Three
The Body in Today's
Reproductive Crisis

Changing our body, regaining control over our sexuality and reproductive capacity, is to change the material conditions of our lives. To what extent this principle must guide our individual and collective activities is shown by the crisis that we are currently experiencing in the US despite the intense feminist activism of the last half of the century. It is a crisis that has many dimensions: sexual, procreative, ecological, medical, cognitive, all rooted however in economic and social developments that have drastically reduced the time and resources at our disposal and increased our anxiety about the future and the violence to which we are exposed. Capitalism's old dream to lengthen the workday, reduce wages, and maximize the unpaid labor accumulated is fully realized today in the United States. Indeed, what Marx described as the "general law of capital accumulation"[1]—the relative impoverishment of workers, the constant creation of surplus/disposable populations, the deskilling of most available jobs, overwork in the presence of a massive number of unemployed "compe[lling] those who are employed to furnish more labor" (Marx 1990, 793)—is the tendency governing economic and social life, and so are the attendant problems of mass indigence, homelessness, and the deepening of inequalities and institutional violence.

Life, indeed, for the majority of people, and women above all, approximates today the Hobbesian description of the state of nature: it is nasty, brutish, and short. Well-to-do Americans may now live into their nineties, but for the rest of us life expectancy is declining, with suicides and deaths from drug overdose also at a record high.[2] Suicides are growing among all sectors of the population, women included. There were over forty-seven thousand recorded suicides in 2017 in the United States, and we will never know how many—among older people—have let themselves die, unrecorded, because a life spent battling with poverty and isolation had no meaning for them. Added to the thousands of deaths from drug overdose, gun violence, police killing, and untreated diseases, they form a worrisome landscape that we cannot ignore in our political work.

In this context, I want to highlight those aspects of this crisis that are particularly relevant for rethinking a feminist agenda. The first are overwork, debt, lack of security, life as constant tension and exhaustion, always thinking of the next task, resulting in health problems, depression, and, as we have seen, an increase in the number of suicides.

Contrasting with the congratulatory, celebratory appraisals, by the United Nations and liberal feminist organizations, of the great steps toward emancipation women have presumably made, the situation today of the majority of the female population could not be bleaker. Undoubtedly, today we are much less tied to the family and to men than in the past. The traditional family is no longer the norm: marriage is at a record low, and most women today have a waged job or even two, even when they have young children. But we are paying a high price for the relative autonomy we have gained. Nothing has changed in the workplace. As we know, most jobs assume that workers are free from family commitments or have someone at home taking care of housework. But as 40 percent of women are the sole providers for their families and the rest have partners who are also employed, domestic work does not disappear when we work outside the home. It is done at night, on weekends, at times that should be devoted to resting and other activities. This means that for many women the workweek averages from sixty to ninety hours, like at the peak of the Industrial Revolution, starting at six in the morning and ending at nine in the evening. Reports abound of women saying that they have hardly any time for themselves and live on the verge of a nervous breakdown, constantly worrying, constantly feeling rushed, anxious, or guilty, especially for not having enough time with the children, or having stress-related health problems starting with depression. Even so, most women have had to reduce the amount of housework they do, which means that essential tasks go unattended, as no services have replaced the work once done by them. Meanwhile programs that could address these problems are being cut.

One would hope that the crisis on the domestic front may be compensated by the satisfactions women may gain from employment. But for most women, working outside the home means to be imprisoned in jobs that destroy their bodies and minds—jobs where you stand up, all day, in shops, airports, and supermarkets, often alone waiting for clients, selling goods that salaries cannot buy, or being chained to a computer screen in box-like, windowless offices. It means paying for daycare and transport and having to depend on fast food at a time when we should be vigilant, given the spread of pesticides and transgenic products and the growth of obesity all around us, including among children. Add that many jobs do not provide paid sick leave or paid maternity leave and that the cost of daycare averages $10,000 a year.

This is not to say that we should not take jobs outside the home. But it is to recognize that "choice" and control over our bodies cannot be achieved only by reducing the number of the children we have or gaining the right not to have children and working for a wage. It is building the power to force the state to relinquish the resources that we need for our families and communities, so that we do not have to take two jobs, spend all our time worrying about money, or give up our children in surrogacy or adoption because we cannot support them. "Going out of the home" and "fighting for equality" is not enough. We must reappropriate resources, work less, regain control of our lives, and take responsibility for the well-being of a broader world than that of our families.

Adding to economic poverty is the poverty of living in a world in which, wherever we turn, we see signs of death. The birds are leaving our skies, rivers are turning into chemical dumps, we have no time for love, friendship, and learning. Capitalism has made us lose sight of the magic of life. In a meeting I met a woman who works as a doula.[3] This is a practice that comes from the reproductive justice movement. It is the idea that women who have a history of mistreatment by the medical profession should not to go the hospital to give birth alone but should go with an advocate. It is a step toward reconstituting the community of women that was once present at the time of birth. This woman was asked, "What is magic?" And her answer was: "Go to see a woman giving birth. There's nothing more magical: the way the rhythms of the mother coordinate with the rhythms of the child is simply magical." But today we give birth on an assembly line. As Meg Fox (1989, 125–29) described it in her article on subjective and objective time in childbirth, today "the time of labor is counted." Labor has become "mere production." The emphasis is on efficiency, as in a time-motion study. Births are not felt. Children are pulled out of sensationless bodies. Giving birth is reduced to a mechanical process.

Nature too is magical. One day the soil is brown and next flowers are generated from it of all colors. How these colors or the forms of the flowers were produced by this same soil no science has yet explained. Magic is the world seen in all its creativity and self-movement. It is around us, but we do not recognize it. We have lost the capacity to relate to it. Attraction among people is also magical. Renaissance scholars spoke of the "harmony of the spheres." They believed that the universe was kept together by an amorous force—similar in its effects to the force of gravity. They believed that the power of "attraction" kept everything in its place and this was as present among humans as it was among the stars. This view of the universe as something living, where everything is interconnected gives power to our struggle. It is an antidote against the cynical view that it is worthless to strive to change the world because "it is too late," "things are too far gone," and we should not get too close to others because we cannot trust them and should think of ourselves first.

Efforts to recuperate our relation with others and with nature are not missing. Women, especially those from indigenous communities, are forming urban gardens, seed banks, they bury their placentas in the earth to remind their children of their ties with the soil. In the US as well, in urban settings, gardens as well as time banks are spreading and other forms of "commoning" once limited to radical groups. We are becoming aware that when we lose our relation to the land we lose much more than an economic resource. As Native Americans have always known, in losing the land we lose our knowledge, our history, our culture. As Marx (1988, 75–76) recognized, nature is our inorganic body, an extension of ourselves. Thus, the death of the earth is our death. When a forest is cut, when the seas are polluted and thousands of whales come to the shore, we too die. Thus, there are now many women's organizations that are working to recuperate older forms of knowledge about herbs and plants.

There is also a growing awareness of the barbaric suffering that is inflicted on animals in almost every branch of industry. Animals too are being turned into machines. In barns across the country that now resemble industrial plants or, more appropriately, animal concentration camps, the lights are kept on day and night so that chickens will produce greater volumes of eggs. It is the same with female pigs. Millions of animals are raised solely to be eaten. They are not seen as living beings but meat producing machines, engineered in such a way that some will never get up on their feet before being driven to a slaughterhouse because the flesh in their bodies is heavier than their legs can support.[4] No wonder we have so many cancers. We live in a poisoned earth and feed on animals that since their birth have been horribly tortured—taking into our own bodies all the poison that their agony has produced.

As I said, we are beginning to develop a revulsion against the Nazi-like cruelty that is inflicted on millions of living beings in the name of satisfying our desires. The rise of Animal Liberation has been an important contribution to revolutionary politics, and so is the silent revolution taking place among many young people across the world who are turning vegetarian or vegan, some perhaps out of concern for their well-being but many out of revulsion against the suffering that the satisfaction of our desire for meat requires.

Yet much remains to be done. Despite so many social movements, social struggles, and so much celebration of human rights, we have not been able to address the main crisis on which American society has been built—the consequences of centuries of slavery and genocide, which like an ocean of blood affects and distorts everything that is done on this continent. What would a feminist movement be like that placed not just the struggle against racism, but also against the institutions that generate it, at the top of its agenda as an intolerable social crime?

Racism in all its forms is so deeply ingrained in white American and European society that extirpating it will require a long revolutionary process. But a feminist movement can mobilize against the policies and institutions that support racial discrimination and the new forms of enslavement to which not only black people but also Latino and immigrant communities are subjected. We also need a movement fighting for the abolition of the death penalty as well as the carceral system and the militarism permeating every aspect of our lives. A feminist objective must be also the liberation of the thousands of women incarcerated in the US—the largest percentage of female prisoners in any country, who are imprisoned mostly for "survival crimes," such as selling sex or forging checks, and because pregnancy, in the case of low-income women and black women, has been increasingly criminalized.

We need a feminist movement that mobilizes in solidarity with our children, whose lives are also daily threatened. There is now some concern for the senseless shootings of kids of all ages in schools and kindergartens, though not enough clearly to change policies relating to gun control. Also, the abuses perpetrated for decades by priests in churches and sacristies are receiving some attention. But feminists have yet to mobilize against the violence to which children are routinely subjected by state institutions, often under the guise of protecting children from their parents, and in the home.

If we refuse the violence done to us, with more reasons we must refuse the violence done to our children. We need to valorize our children, looking at them as companions rather than inferior beings. Children have not yet interiorized the defeats and conventions that shape our relations with others as we become adults and can spot immediately what is false, artificial. Only through years of conditioning do we learn to hide and simulate. Thus, there is much we can learn from them.

Putting an end to all forms of violence done to children is an urgent matter, as childhood is in a state of emergency in the US schools are becoming prisons, with metal detectors and guards at the door. Creative programs are eliminated from their curricula, at least in the public schools. And at home there is less and less time for children. We should not be surprised, then, if they are unhappy and rebel. Instead this rebellion is described as mental illness and medicalized. This is easier and more profitable than recognizing the reasons for children's discontent. It would be a revolution indeed if, instead of spending a trillion dollars to refurbish the nuclear system, the US government spent a trillion dollars to make sure that our schools stimulate the creativity of our children. This is a good feminist project and a good feminist demand!

Notes

1   Marx, *Capital*, vol. 1, pt. 7, chap. 25.
2   As reported by Shehab Khan, in the *Independent* (November 29, 2018) "Suicides in the US hit a record level in years, prompting a decline in life expectancy." Deaths due to overdose also climbed, surpassing seventy thousand in 2017. According to the Center for Disease Control and Prevention, up to seven hundred thousand people in the United States died from a drug overdose between 1999 and 2017, involving opioids. Every day an average of 130 people die of overdose.
3   On the significance of the role of doulas as advocated for women giving birth, see Alana Apfel, *Birth Work as Care Work* (2016)
4   A powerful, poignant denunciation of the cruelties inflicted on animals in the industrial farms where they are raised by the thousands before being brought to the slaughterhouse is in Sunaura Taylor's *Beasts of Burden* (2017), which, while exposing the living hell on which the food industry is built, shows that the degradation of animals "has contributed to unspeakable violence against humans" (107).

PART TWO

FOUR

On the Body, Gender, and Performance

Can gender be considered a product of "performance"? This assumption is now popular among feminists in the US and for reasons that are easy to understand. Describing a gender category like "woman" as the product of performance means rejecting centuries of restrictions and rules imposed on us by appeal to a mythical female nature. Echoing Simone de Beauvoir's (1989, 267) statement that "one is not born, but rather becomes, a woman," performance theory appears to be on a continuum with the 1970s feminist insistence on the socially constructed character of "femininity." There are, however, differences that should be noted, as they point to the theoretical limits of this concept. Whether we assumed that the normative definition of "femininity" was a product of "patriarchy" or we saw it rooted in the capitalist exploitation of female labor, our critique of it always investigated and named the sources of women's oppression, as we looked for political strategies that would transform not only our lives but also society as a whole. Identifying, naming, analyzing the source of the "norms" to which we were expected to conform was important also to demonstrate the complex nature of "gender construction." It was important to show that our acceptance of the rules and regulations institutionally prescribed was always more than an acting out of the "norm," as "performance" implies. Most often it would be an involuntary submission, accompanied by an inner sense of injustice and desire for revolt, very formative, we discovered, of what "woman" came to mean to us.

Performance is a useful concept. But its range of application is a limited, partial one. The concept suggests passive obedience to a law, enactment of a norm, an act of consent. In this was social identification as woman becomes almost inevitably a self-inflicted wound. It overlooks that gender is the result of a long process of disciplining and that it is maintained not simply through the imposition of "norms" but through the organization of work, the division of labor, the setting up of differentiated labor markets, and the organization of the family, sexuality, and domestic work. In each of these contexts what is often called "performance" would more properly be defined as coercion and exploitation. We do not "perform" gender by working as a nurse, a sex worker, a waitress, a mother, or a paid care worker. Describing our production of femininity in such occupations as "performance" greatly reduces our understanding of the actual dynamics, it hides the economic compulsion involved and the fact that, beneath the appearance of compliance, practices of resistance and refusal are nourished that undermine what the performance was expected to consolidate. This is not to exclude that in performing these jobs we may become so identified with them that our whole persona is reshaped by them. Paraphrasing Jean-Paul Sartre's comments in his analysis of "bad faith," the public demands of these workers that they play femininity through these particular forms of work. Indeed, many precautions are taken to imprison a woman in what she is supposed to be, "as if we lived in perpetual fear that that [she] might escape from it, that [she] might break away and suddenly elude [her] condition."[1]

Yet we do break away. The rise of the women's liberation movement would be incomprehensible if the concept of "performance" were our main guideline, with its implications of passive reception and reproduction of normative standards. Emerging at the end of one of the most repressive decades in

American history, from the viewpoint of gender formation and discipline, the women's liberation movement would have to be a mystery if we missed the deep-seated rebellion brewing under the appearances of conformity and—equally important—the fact that this rebellion was not a rejection of gender as such but a rejection of a specific, devaluing definition of womanhood that the women's movement put to death despite many institutional attempts to preserve it.

There are two points, then, I would like to stress. First, performance helps us to denaturalize "femininity." It extends our appreciation of the socially constructed character of gender identities and values, but it does not allow us to acknowledge that for social/gender change to occur we need to transform not only our individual and collective vision of gender but also the institutions by which gender relations have been perpetuated, starting with the sexual division of labor and the social hierarchies constructed on the devaluation of reproductive work. Second, performance flattens the content of social action, suggesting that the only alternatives open to us are consent or dissent, thereby underestimating the rebellion brewing in many acts of consent—the many forms of sabotage built under our apparent yessing the system, which, under particular historical conditions, can turn into powerful movements.

These considerations have an immediate bearing on two other issues that also play a large role in today's radical politics. The first is the question of "identity" and "identity politics." This is an issue that has belabored feminists for years, raising a chorus of critiques that could have been directed more appropriately against other targets. As with "performance," under the concept of "identity" structural elements of the capitalist system in which we live are hidden and so is the incessant process of struggle by which they are eroded.

Clearly "black," as in Black Power, "black liberation," "black is beautiful," is an identity, but what it stands for is a history of exploitation and struggle. "Black" is certainly not the identity of the passport, the registry office, an identity that freeze us and pins against a wall. It is not the identity of which John Locke ([1689] 1959, 1:458–59) spoke in his work as constitutive of the person, which, he noted, postulates the sameness of the self and is the foundation for the possibility of punishment. *It is an identity that is collective and embraced through a process of struggle*. This is to say that social identities are not only jails in which a hegemonic system imprisons us, and they are not garments which we cannot tear, turn upside down, discard. Viewing social identities as unilaterally constructed, ignoring the capacity that we have to change our social identity, to turn labels intended to vilify us into badges of pride is to assume the inevitability of defeat, it is to see power only on the side of the master.

The same case can be made for "women" as a social identity.

If "women" is not a biological concept, if it is a social construction, then the question to be asked is: what does it stand for and who are the actors involved in the process of its constitution? Who has the power to define what "women" means? And how is the normative meaning challenged by the struggles that women are making.

For those of us who did not accept that being born with a uterus and having the capacity to procreate was necessarily a condemnation to a life of subordination, the alternative was to seek an answer in the history, past and present, of the exploitation of human labor. Thus, "women" for us defined above all a particular place, a particular function in the capitalist division of labor, but also, at the same time, a battle cry, as fighting against that definition also changed its content.

In other words, "woman" is not a static, monolithic term but one that has simultaneously different, even opposite and always changing significations. It is not just a performance, an embodiment of institutional norms, but also a contested terrain, constantly being fought over and redefined.

Last, performance theory has generated the idea that our physiological constitution is of little relevance to our social experience. From the incontrovertible fact that we apprehend our biology through cultural filters and "biology" itself is directly affected by sociocultural factors, all too often it is deduced that the material constitution of our bodies is a subject matter of which it is better not to speak. My reference here is less to the theory of performance articulated, for example, by Judith Butler, at least in her later works, than to the popular version of it circulating among feminists. Here too I first wish to clear the ground from possible misunderstandings. I agree with Donna Haraway that "biology is politics," though I attribute a different meaning to this statement. I believe it is politics because it has so persistently and so negatively been used against us that it is almost impossible to speak of "biology" in a neutral way, without fear of reinforcing the existing prejudices. It is also politics because decisions concerning the most significant factors in the constitution and development of our physical makeup have been made in institutional contexts (universities, medical labs, etc.) beyond our control, prompted by economic and political interests, and because we know that though our bodies are the products of a long evolutionary process, they have nevertheless been impacted by a host of policies that have constantly modified them even at the level of the DNA. In other words, "bodies" and "nature" have a history; they are not a raw bedrock on which cultural meaning are attached.

Environmental and nutritional policies have been responsible for many mutations our bodies have undergone, like those we are plausibly experiencing at present because of our increasing exposure to radiation. Indeed, no pristine, immutable nature speaks through our bodies and our actions. At the same time, it would be absurd to dismiss some key aspects of our embodiment as socially not significant only because of their "contamination" by social, historical, and cultural practices. The fact that we cannot apprehend the world that we inappropriately call nature, biology, the body, except through a screen of social values, interests, and political considerations, and the fact that "nature" and "physiology" have a history does not imply that we must rule them out of our discourse, and that all that we can speak about are purely culturally produced realities that we have the power of making and unmaking.

Whether or not, in some future time, we can erase death from the human condition and, like trees, live until our physical frame breaks down, the fact remains that death is currently our inevitable companion, a significant fact in our lives, regardless of how we culturally experience it and live it. The same is true for birth-giving and maternity, which, once stripped of their compulsory character and hypocritical celebrations, remain for a large part of the world population, and women first of all, life-defining events. I must add that I have a great sympathy for the reluctance with which so many women confront this subject, which remains a booby-trapped terrain. But blanketing maternity, by being silent about it, for fear of boosting the power of the right-to-lifers or reinforcing naturalizing conceptions of femininity, is in fact precluding the very process by which the creativity of these experiences can be recuperated.

Paradoxically, a testimony to the relevance of difference in our experience of our physical makeup comes from a large section of the trans movement that is strongly committed to a constructivist view of gender identities, as many undergo costly and dangerous surgeries and medical treatments in order to transition to a different gender.

It is, moreover, by deciding not to ignore the material/physiological aspect of our bodies that we can challenge the dominant reductive conception of gender and recognize the broad range of possibilities that "nature" provides. On this basis, already the intersex movement has shown that intersex people are not a mere literary figure or a rare phenomenon, for a considerable number of children are born with undefined sexual characteristics.[2] This means that we are already moving toward the recognition of a third gender or more genders for what until now was a secret of the birth room, rapidly and cruelly corrected by doctors committed to sexual dimorphism, is now becoming fully visible as it has been already in different societies and cultures. In this case too, however, preventing the doctors' knives from regulating intersex bodies can only be a beginning—for the overcoming of gender as a disciplinary tool and a means of exploitation will require reappropriating the control over our lives and our reproduction. This means going beyond the body even though the body—as women in Latin America have so often insisted—remains the primary territory of encounter with the world and the primary object of our defense.

Notes

1   Jean-Paul Sartre, "Bad Faith" in *Being and Nothingness* (1956), 102. Using the example of a waiter in a café, a grocer, or a tradesman, Sartre stresses how their performance appears as a game, a ceremony, yet a very serious one, because the public demands that they realize it. Thus "there is the dance of the grocer, of the tailor, of the auctioneer, by which they endeavor to persuade their clientele that they are nothing but a grocer, a tailor, an auctioneer. . . . There are indeed many precautions to imprison a man in what he is, as if we lived in perpetual fear that he might escape from it, that he might break away and suddenly escape his condition" (102). "Bad faith" for Sartre comes into play when we forget that we are not "the person we have to be." His concern in fact is that we recognize our ontological capacity to transcend the identities we are compelled to perform.
2   On this subject see the classic work of Anne Fausto-Sterling, *Sexing the Body* (2000).

FIVE

Remaking Our Bodies, Remaking the World?

The idea of remaking our bodies is a very old one, and so has been our desire to break free from its limits, for example, by acquiring animal powers like the capacity to fly. Indeed, throughout history human beings have remade their bodies and those of others by means of facial marks, cranial modifications, muscle building, and tattoos. This for sake of group identification, to project personal or collective power, to beautify themselves.[1] Bodies are also texts on which power regimes have written their prescriptions. As the point of encounter with the human and nonhuman world, the body has been our most powerful means of self-expression and the most vulnerable to abuse. Thus, our bodies are evidence of the pains and joys we have experienced and the struggles we have made. Histories of oppression and rebellion can be read through them.

Never before in history, however, has the possibility of changing our bodies been so close to realization and an object of such intense desire. Running in a park in the morning or walking by a gym at night, one has the impression of a mass movement, eliciting the kind of passion in the past reserved for political meetings. Hordes of people every morning crowd the parks, running in groups, in twos, individually, or they bicycle or walk; meanwhile gyms are contributing to the change of the urban landscape with their impressive displays of metallic instruments and laboring bodies, now increasingly covered by tattoos, sometimes covering the whole body as if with a new skin. And this is only a part—the low-tech part—of the remakes. At the high-tech level, the sense that we are entering a new era is even more pronounced. Because of the new reproductive technologies, women can extend their generative time and have children after menopause or delegate to other women the task of procreating "their children." Through gene editing—still at an experimental stage—doctors promise to eliminate at birth all bodily inscribed propensities to illness. And with the implant of microchips, a new world is coming into existence of supermen and women, waving their hands to unlock their cars and enter buildings and carrying their vital data encoded into their bodies. With powers once the subject of mythology,[2] surgeons are now remaking gender, while even bolder scientists fantasize about a day when remakes will leave the body behind, transcend it, discard it, to relocate our minds in less perishable electronic circuits.[3] Meanwhile, plastic and cosmetic surgeries are at an all-time high, especially used by women. Millions of noses, lips, breasts, even vaginal labia are being remodeled, wrinkles are being smoothed from aging foreheads, and the trend is growing.[4]

What Does the Present Popularity of Body Remakes Signify?

What does this tell us about the changing conception of our bodies? And what are the "body politics" of this phenomenon?

Clearly body remakes fulfill many people's needs and desires. In a world where at every turn we face competition and constantly undergo an experience of devaluation, body remakes are important as means of self-valorization. "Remaking" our bodies is also a necessity in a context in which families and health-care systems can be counted upon less and less to address our bodily crises. Mindful of the social and monetary cost of disease and the fact that no one is any longer there for us—since parents, lovers, friends are all over-extended and living at the limits of their capacities—we diet, jog, bicycle, crowd fitness joints, meditate. It is our responsibility, we are told, if we get sick. Doctors do not ask us whether we live close to a chemical dump or have money problems, but how many drinks we have, how many cigarettes we smoke, how many miles we run. Social pressure is also a factor. Though no union contract stipulates it, staying healthy and having a good appearance is now an unsigned job requirement and a point in our favor at an interview or a date.

Necessity, however, is only one side of the present craze for remakes. Desire is even more important.

As difficult and costly as they may be, cosmetic surgery, pharmacological therapies, and other forms of body remake may offer a more promising solution—to those who can afford them—than waiting for the development of an egalitarian society where appearance no longer matters. On the other hand, the politics of body remakes is in several ways problematic. Besides the danger of medical speculation and malpractice, there is the further concern that body remakes remain individual solutions and add to the process of social stratification and exclusion, as the "care of the body" requires more money, time, and access to services and resources than the majority can afford, particularly when surgeries are involved. Already images are jarring. While the bodies of some are becoming more fit, more perfect, the number of those who can hardly move because of excess weight, illness, and poor nutrition is growing. *Bodies and worlds are drifting apart.*

This is where a new "body politics" is in order, helping us devise how the management of our bodies and their remakes may fit in a broader process of social emancipation, so that our strategies for survival do not give more power to the social forces that are sending many of us to die, and they do not contribute to a well-being whose price and content distance us from other people.

For women the added danger is acceptance of an aesthetic discipline that in the 1970s we rejected. In the feminist movement we refused to be divided into beautiful and ugly and to conform to the latest model of beauty imposed on us, which we often pursued with painful diets at the cost of our health.[5] Moreover, with the rise of feminism, as with the rise of Black Power, beauty too was redefined. We saw each other as beautiful because we were defiant, because in freeing ourselves from the prescriptions of a misogynous society we explored new ways of being, new ways of laughing, hugging, wearing our hair, crossing our legs, new ways of being together and making love.

We also had a healthy distrust of the medical profession that today holds for many the hope of a rebirth.[6] Possibly because many doctors now are women, the fear of medicine as a state institution has receded. With the development of biotechnologies, doctors today even appear as benevolent magicians holding the keys to not only our well-being but also metamorphoses that will revolutionize our lives. Yet while we have many well-meaning and caring doctors, medicine as an institution continues to be at the service of power and the market, and we would do well not to forget its history as an instrument of capital's incessant attempt to refurbish our humanity and break down our resistance to exploitation. Indeed, a whole history of medicine could be written from the viewpoint of its disciplinary function. From the massive sterilization programs implemented at the service of eugenics, to the invention of lobotomies, electroshocks, and psychoactive drugs, the history of medicine has consistently displayed a will to social control and determination to reprogram our refractory bodies so as to make us more docile and productive.

For instance, not only have doctors waged a war on intersex people, lesbians and gays, as well as on women refusing the discipline of housework. In the 1950s, black people of all ages and children classified as retarded were subjected to terrifying experiments, even involving the repeated injection of radioactive material in the veins of unsuspecting black adults and children.[7] It is remarkable that none of the doctors who led such experiments were reprimanded or had to suffer the penal consequences of their behavior, whereas at Nuremberg Nazi scientists were condemned to death for similar crimes. On the contrary, some built brilliant careers through such programs (Hornblum et al. 2013, 155, 176).

Even at its best, medicine and medical practice are mined terrains, responding more to the needs of insurance companies, funding sources, and career building than our actual well-being, and promising solutions that often turn against us. Consider the still-ongoing terror campaign organized to warn us about faulty genes in our DNA,[8] ready to spring on us and send us to our graves. So terrifying this campaign has been that already women have been convinced to undergo preventive radical mastectomies, a traumatic procedure, of unknown consequences, likely to endanger their health more than the evolution of the faulty genes they presumably carry. Meanwhile, our waters, foods, and air are more and more contaminated; our stress, and indeed desperation, in the face of overwork, lack of hopes for the future, and the precarization of our existence are escalating. Allergies never before experienced by previous generations have reached epidemic proportions—all without the medical profession denouncing these well-understood causes of our morbidities and forcefully organizing to demand change. Women have been particularly affected by the irresponsible way in which doctors have approached the care of our bodies. Think of the many who have developed cancers due to doctor-approved silicone implants that were to reconstitute their breasts and also of the reckless dissemination of contraceptives like Depo Provera and Norplant that are demonstrably destructive of women's health, functioning more as instruments of social control than as means of self-determinations. Think of the proliferation of unnecessary cesarean births, and these are only very few examples.

Capital's Cartesian Dream

Furthermore, as Finn Bowring has well argued in his *Science, Seeds and Cyborgs* (2003), we are entering a new phase in which the creation of an "immaterial" human being, freed from the impediments posed by a finite biological frame constructed over billions of years. In sum, the creation of a disembodied humanity is now openly upheld as a social ideal. As Bowring, among others, points out, this new venture is not occurring in a vacuum. Since the 1980s, mechanical conceptions of the body as a patchwork of decentered mechanisms, open to be rearranged according to our will and desire, have circulated through philosophy, sociology, and even feminist theory. From the necessary rejection of the nature/culture dichotomy, conceptions of biology as something that can be rearranged or remade have been spawned, that affect our understanding of the consequences of the medical experimentation with our bodies. Thus, if Bowring's analysis is correct, cloning, gene editing, and gene transferring are all on the agenda for human remake, after having been applied already to the creation of new breeds of plants and animals.[9] A thrust of scientific research is directed to devising ways to emancipate us from the limits imposed on our action and apprehension by biology itself, for instance by enhancing the power of the brain by means of electronic prostheses enabling us to think and read faster, store more memory, and depend less and less on the physical conditions of our corporeal structure, such as the periodic need for food and sleep.

No doubt only a select part of the population would qualify for such upgrading. If the global organization of production is any indication, capital accumulation still needs warm bodies to exploit, including those of children, backward as they may be, from the viewpoint of capital's dream of a world of cyborgs. But modifying or replacing our old/finite bodies with technological alternatives is becoming an impellent necessity as capitalist planners (and some leftists too) look at space as a new frontier of production, and program machines are being produced that are fast outpacing our capacities to use them. In sum, Dr. Frankenstein's dream is back on the table, not only in the form of a human-shaped robot, but also as a technologically enhanced human being of the kind that the implantation of microchips in our bodies is already preparing.

Remaking Our Bodies or Remaking Medicine?

Whatever the extent and the pace of the anticipated changes may be, we can be certain that doctors will be protagonists in this process, and we must therefore be concerned that medical research seemingly directed to other aims may be instrumental to the making of a self-induced evolutionary leap in the constitution of our corporeal reality that will not likely be inspired by the desire to improve our well-being. As demonstrated by the history of eugenics and the atrocious experiments on black people and even children that reached a peak during the Cold War and after, medicine in the US has a dark history that should make us cautious of the gifts it promises to us and the power it receives from our consent.

We must, then, avoid making the medical profession the godlike creators of our bodies and instead direct our activism to devising ways in which we can exercise some control over our encounters with it. There are many examples of this. In the middle of the nineteenth century a Popular Health Movement developed in the US that encouraged people to develop their own medical knowledge, as it looked at official medicine with suspicion as an elite, undemocratic operation.[10] In the 1970s, feminists in Chicago and other parts of the country set up underground clinics to practice abortion, in case it continued to be outlawed. Later in the 1980s ACT UP (AIDS Coalition to Unleash Power), responding to the lack of attention by the Reagan administration to the AIDS crisis, created a remarkable network of doctors, researchers, care workers, as well as gay activists seeking new cures, pressuring the pharma companies internationally to lower the prices of lifesaving medicines, in the process showing to the world their determination and capacity to care for their gay brothers. Both the feminist self-help movement and ACT UP had a powerful influence on official medicine, again setting an example of what care can be. As the medical technologies apt to remake our bodies expand, understanding what effects they will have on our health, what advantages they do procure, to what extent we truly need them or whether we are being used as experimental subjects become question of great urgency. Few of such initiatives today exist. The experience of ACT UP has not been replicated. Exception made for a growing network of black women's health projects, the mobilization around the care of the body is mostly organized from above—see the many marches and marathons for cancer treatment, breast cancer, and so forth—mobilizing us to send funds to various institutions but failing to expand our knowledge of what can be done to prevent the disease.

In conclusion, our relation to the making and unmaking of our bodies—whether in the treatment of diseases, cosmetic remodeling, or more structural remakes—we are dependent on an institution that is guided by commercial and governmental principles. Yet there is a possibility of sharing medical knowledge, concerns, and fears with others in neighborhoods and towns and connecting with willing nurses and doctors working within the institutions, and this possibility should be developed, so that we can build a collective understanding of what is involved in the transformations to which we submit our bodies and a collective power to gain the medical care we need. Certainly, becoming participants in decision making that deeply affects our lives and defending such decisions from commercial consideration or experimentation on humans will bring a change in our lives more profound than those produced by any remaking of the body.

Notes

1   On this subject, see Polhemus (1978).

2   I am referring here to the legend narrated in Plato's *Symposium*, which describes Apollo dividing, cutting in two, god-defying, primeval beings and then, like a modern surgeon, turning their genitals around, sewing them up here and there, and crafting human beings in the form that we know, incomplete, missing their amputated part, perennially looking for the other half.

3   See Finn Bowring, *Science, Seeds and Cyborgs* (2003), especially chap. 11: "The Cyborg Solution."

4   Facial cosmetic surgery is far more common today than in the 1990s and not only as an antiaging remedy. Chiara Townley writes in *Medical News* (March 17, 2019), "Cosmetic Surgery Is on the Rise, New Data Reveal." Though the majority of those who seek cosmetic surgery are women, the number of men who do it is also deemed "significant." https://www.medicalnewstoday.com/articles/324693. php.

      See also Brandon Baker, "Is Facial Plastic Surgery Still Popular?," *Philly Voice*, July 12, 2018, https://www.phillyvoice.com/plastic-surgery-still-popular-beauty-facelift/. According to the American Society of Plastic Surgeons, the demand for body shaping is on the rise. In the US alone 17.5 million people in 2018 underwent minimally invasive plastic and cosmetic surgeries, for a total expense of $16.5 billion. "New Statistics Reveal the Shape of Plastic Surgery," March 1, 2018, https://www.plasticsurgery.org/news/press-releases/new-statistics-reveal-the-shape-of-plastic-surgery.

5   On this subject see the excellent book by Susan Bordo, *Unbearable Weight* (1993).

6   The intensity and power of that distrust was brought back to me by a recent rereading of Barbara Ehrenreich and Deirdre English, *Witches, Midwives and Nurses* (2010), which powerfully illustrates how the history of the rise of the medical profession occurred, at all stages, through the suppression of women's healing practices, accomplished through the persecution of healers as witches and the displacement of midwives, and was an instrument of the social disciplining of women.

7   On this topic, in addition to James H. Jones, *Bad Blood* (1993), see A.M. Hornblum, Judith L. Newman, and Gregory J. Dober, *Against their Will: The Secret History of Medical Experimentation on Children in Cold War America* (2013); and Eileen Welsome, *The Plutonium Experiment* (1993).

8   Again, in August 2019, the National Cancer Institute issued guidelines urging women who have had breast cancer to take BRCA tests to assess their risk level for breast and ovarian cancer, despite much

evidence that breast cancer is most likely caused by environmental factors like the high dosages of pesticides present (for a start) in the food and water we consume.

9   On the creation of animals with new characteristics through the transfer and injection of DNA from animals of different species, see Bowring (2003), 117–22.

10 For an extensive discussion of the Popular Health Movement and its relation to feminist activism, see Ehrenreich and English (2010), 69–74. Ehrenreich and English write that "women were the backbone" of the movement, whose practice emphasize preventive care rather than therapy, and a democratization of medical knowledge. Thus, "Ladies Physiological Societies" "sprang up everywhere" instructing women in "anatomy and personal hygiene" with the assumption that every person should be their own doctor (69). See also Paul Starr (1982).

SIX

Surrogate Motherhood: A Gift of Life or Maternity Denied?

The charge that capitalism has turned women's bodies into machines for the production of labor power has been a central theme of feminist literature since the 1970s. Yet the advent of surrogate motherhood is a turning point in this process, as it represents gestation as a purely mechanical process, as alienated labor, in which the woman hired must have no emotional involvement. Surrogacy is also a new turn from the viewpoint of the commodification of human life, as it is the organization and legitimation of a children's market, and the definition of child as a property that can be transferred, bought, and sold. This, in fact, is the essence of "surrogate motherhood," a practice that is now widespread in several countries, starting with the United States, but continues to be enveloped in a cloud of mystification.

As the Italian feminist sociologist Daniela Danna points out in her *Contract Children* (2015), the very concept of "surrogacy" is deceptive, for it suggests that the "birthing mother" is not the real one, but it is only "an aid, a helper," and what she does is on behalf of the "real mother"—the provider of the egg which the surrogate then transforms into a child. Justification for this terminology comes from the new reproductive technologies—in vitro fertilization (IVF) and embryo transfer—which generate the illusion that the owners of the implanted egg have property rights over the child, since the gestational mother is genetically unrelated to it. As Danna comments, this is a fallacious argument that can only be maintained through an abstract conception of property, ignoring that the "birthing mother" is the one who materially creates and nourishes the child, a process that entails not only nine months of labor but a transference of genetic material, as the child is truly made from her flesh and bones (68).

It is thanks to this mystification and to the development of a supporting commercial and institutional machine, made of insurance companies, doctors, and lawyers, that over the last three decades surrogacy has greatly expanded. Currently thousands of children are born every year in this way, and in some countries "baby farms" have opened, where "surrogate mothers" are inseminated and reside throughout their pregnancy. In India, for instance, prior to the ban on transnational surrogacy in 2015, three thousand such clinics existed (Vora 2019), providing the infrastructure for a breeding industry, in which the constitution of the woman's body into a procreative machine was nearly complete.

Problems nevertheless remain. In most countries of the European Community surrogacy is still formally forbidden or is subjected to limits and regulations. In the Netherlands, for instance, the surrogate mother is given a few weeks after delivery to decide whether she wants to separate from the child. But as Danna, among others, points out, restrictions are increasingly being eroded, and, far from limiting the practice, regulation is becoming the fastest path to its legal recognition.

Among the principles used to overcome existing prohibitions in disputed cases, or to facilitate the legal recognition of children acquired through surrogacy abroad, is that the decision should be made in "the best interest of the child." This, however, is an expedient to bypass the law and a legitimation of the classist and racist implications of this practice, as the interest of affluent white couples is always prioritized in the assignation of the child.

Appeal is also made to the compelling nature of the "contracts" that oblige surrogate mothers to consign the child upon delivery. Surrogacy, indeed, is an outstanding example of how the law is playing crucial role in the upholding of neoliberal reform, as contracts are conferred a sacred status with little consideration given to the conditions under which they were made. Yet, as the famous case of "Baby M" made clear,[1] it is difficult for women to anticipate, at the time of signing the contract, how they would feel after experiencing, day after day, for nine months, a new life growing into their wombs. Furthermore, no consideration is given in the stipulation of the contracts to the effects of the separation from the child. Meanwhile, the contracts themselves have become more complex and constraining. They not only oblige the surrogate mother to relinquish the child after birth but also demand a strict control over her daily life during the pregnancy period, with regard to medical treatment, sexual behavior, food intake, and so forth. Not last in the construction of legitimizing arguments, the existence of *a right to parenting* is being legally theorized for which surrogate mothering becomes the indispensable condition. This argument is already used, surprisingly even in radical circles, on behalf of gay male couples, who allegedly must hire a surrogate precisely to realize their presumably absolute paternity rights.

In sum, the writing on the wall points to surrogacy as the wave of the future. But as surrogate mothering is normalized, it is crucial to highlight the classist and racist premises on which it is founded and its destructive consequences for the children thus produced and for women. A worrisome one is the presence of a number of "suspended children," who, having been denied, for various reasons, legal certification in the countries where the "intended" parents reside, or having been born with disabilities, are rejected by both the surrogate mother and the commissioning couple. A Reuters investigative report has also found that through the internet adoptive parents, at least in the US, can dispose of children adopted abroad, without any difficulty, through a practice called "private rehoming" that is totally unregulated.[2] Even more worrisome is the evidence that some surrogate children are channeled to the organs market, for once the transaction has taken place no institutional oversight checks what happens to the children marketed this way, who in most cases are taken to other regions, thousands of miles away from the place of their birth.

Also to be considered is the trauma that the newborns suffer upon separation from the "birthing mother." No sufficient time has passed, since surrogate mothering was introduced, for an adequate body of case histories to have emerged. We know, however, that mother and child know each other long before birth, that at three months after conception the fetus can recognize the mother's voice and that it is so much part of her body that immediately upon birth the infant knows where to look for food and care (Merino 2017). Apparently some babies "can't calm down if kept away from their birth mother," sometimes crying for months (Danna 2015, 63, 65). Seeing one's mother turn over her newborn child to strangers may also have a traumatic impact on her other children, who fear that the same destiny will occur to them.

Surrogate mothers too suffer in this process. Though cases of refusal to separate from the child are apparently rare, some mothers have publicly spoken against it, and more would probably have done so except for the care that organizing agencies have taken to prevent this possibility. By contract surrogate mothers are urged not to develop any feelings for the child they carry, and all measures are taken to limit the contact between them and the newborn. Cesarean deliveries are preferred, so that when the mother wakes up, the child is gone. Her sense of self-importance is also fostered. Her bravery and generosity are praised, and her separation from the child is portrayed as the ultimate test of altruism. She is also constantly reminded that that she has no real relation to the child and that her pregnancy is of a different type, in which the real agents are the doctors and the providers or "donors" of the fertilized egg (Danna 2015, 135). Even so, for many, the sense of loss lingers. This is especially true in the case of women who had no idea of the intensive medical treatments to which they would have to submit and the related risks to their health or those who have entered the contract convinced that they would continue to have a role in the future life of the child and that by giving a child to a well-to-do couple they would develop ties that could benefit the other members of their family (Vora 2019).

Other factors make surrogacy the epitome of the capitalist conception of social relations. While defenders portray it as a humanitarian gesture, a gift of life enabling couples who cannot have children to experience the joys of parenting, the fact is that it is women from the poorest regions of the world who generally take on this task, and surrogacy would not exist except for the monetary compensations it fetches. Quite properly, then, in "Surrogates and Outcast Mothers: Racism and Reproductive Politics in the Nineties" (1993), Angela Davis has argued that surrogacy is continuous with the breeding practices that were enforced on the American slave plantations, with poor women in both cases being destined to forfeit their children, once born, for the profit of the rich.

The profound racism inherent to the practice of surrogacy is also underlined by Dorothy Roberts, who in her classic *Killing the Black Body* ([1997] 2017, 250–52), shows how all new reproductive technologies "reinforce a racist standard for procreation." She points out, for instance, that overwhelmingly it is white families who seek surrogates, being obsessively concerned with their genetic heritage and being able to afford the process. Black families, by contrast, tend to have neither the means to pay for surrogate procreation nor the disposition to turn to the medical profession to resolve their problems, in view of all the abuses they may have suffered at the hands of hospital and doctors. They have also a different conception of parenting, developed out of a long history of enslavement and oppression, a conception in which all in the community are responsible for its children and all are sisters and brothers. Indeed, surrogacy is mostly a white practice and an outstanding example of how the right to reproduce ourselves is severely restricted, and again how technology serves to deepen not just specialization but class privileges and differentiations. While medicine is leaving no stone unturned to guarantee nonfertile, well-to-do couples the possibility of having a child, the same right is today denied not only to black people descendent of Africans enslaved but to the many women that international economic policies have impoverished, who must often migrate and leave their children behind to go working in countries where they care for other people's children, or, alternatively, are hounded by international agencies and their local representatives to have contraceptives they cannot control (like Norplant or IUDs) implanted into their bodies to make it impossible for them to procreate. The classist and racist character of surrogate mothering is particularly evident if one sets it side by side with the present "criminalization of pregnancy" in the case of black women in the United States, who once pregnant are exposed to so many charges that, according to national health advocate Lynn Paltrow (2013), they practically fall outside the Constitution.

As with domestic work, in the case of surrogacy as well, we see the emergence of a new sexual division of labor whereby procreation—reduced to a purely mechanical process and stripped of all affective components—is outsourced to women in formerly colonized regions of the world that, since the late 1970s, have been subjected to brutal austerity programs, leading to mass impoverishment and dispossession from the most basic means of reproduction. In this case too, evoking a point often made by Maria Mies (2014), "underdevelopment" in one part of the world is the necessary condition for "development" in another. Women who in the early

1980s would have been accused of overpopulating the world and practically forced to accept sterilization are now put to use, producing children they cannot call their own, once again denied the very right to maternity that is proclaimed as unconditional and legally defended in the case of those who have more monetary resources available to them. There is a stark difference, in fact, in the rhetoric that is used to establish the right of the better-off to reproduce themselves or that is used by scientists, labs, and doctors to guarantee its actualization, and the rhetoric reserved for the surrogate mother, who is contractually expected to expropriate herself of her feelings, emotions, and her very solidarity for the child she carries, as if "it" were a purely physical growth, an object, not worthy of any considerations.

What most condemns surrogate mothering, however, is that it is a further step toward the assumption that human beings can be bought and sold like any other commodity and that children can be produced specifically for that purpose. This is not a novel practice. We are reminded here of Marx's remark concerning the effects of the introduction of machinery in the work process, which incentivized the capitalists to buy children and persons of a young age. This, Marx noted, also changed the relation between parents and their children. "Previously the workman sold his own labour-power, which he disposed of nominally as a free agent. Now he sells wife and child. He has become a slave-dealer" (1:396).

The same can be said of the women who sign surrogacy contracts, who are the last incarnation of a long set of proletarian figures who have looked at children as a means of survival. But what sets surrogate mothering apart is that the sale of the child to another person is for life. This is what distinguishes surrogacy from prostitution, to which it is often compared. For while the prostitute sells to others a service and the temporary use of her body, the surrogate gives to others, in exchange for money, complete control over the life of a child.

Stressing this fact is obviously not intended to raise a moralistic complaint against the women who become surrogates, who often are pushed into this path by family members or have so little access to resources of their own that, as an alternative to a constant battle with survival, consider renting their wombs, in the same way as others may consider selling their kidneys, their hair, their blood. It is a telling sign of the poverty that many surrogate mothers experience that some, when interviewed, described the months of gestation as a vacation, the first they have had in their lives. But we need to unmask the immense hypocrisy of the rhetoric surrounding this practice, which pretends that this is a work of love, a pure expression of altruism, a "gift of life," while erasing the fact that it is done by some of the poorest women in the world and that the beneficiaries are well-to-do couples who, upon acquiring the children, wish to have no relation with the surrogate.

Instead of hypocritically celebrating surrogate mothers' alleged altruism, we should reflect on the abysmal conditions of poverty that lead a woman to accept to carry for nine months a child she will never be allowed to care for and whose destiny she is prohibited to know. We should also be concerned—as many feminists have—that the subdivision and specialization of mothering into gestational, social, biological, represents a devaluation of this process, once considered a power of women, and a restoration of a sexist, patriarchal, truly Aristotelian conception of women's bodies and women themselves, who are portrayed, in the rhetoric of surrogacy, as passive carriers of a life to which they contribute nothing of their own except for "brute matter."

Should surrogacy *not* be legalized? This is an issue that needs to generate more debate than it has so far, as it poses the question of the degree to which we can turn to the state to ensure that our lives are not violated. One argument sometimes raised against it is that legalization offers surrogate mothers some protection, where the criminalization of the practice would expose them to an even higher risk, as the practice would undoubtedly continue clandestinely. It is also dangerous to demand from the state any punitive regulation and intervention, as history shows that such measures are always used against those who are already victimized. How, then, are we to protect the children born from surrogate transactions? What initiatives do we need to take to prevent the generalization of the buying and selling of other people's lives?

Notes

1   "Baby M" was the name given by the court and the media to the child of Mary Beth Whitehead, a surrogate mother in New Jersey, who upon delivery of a baby girl, on March 27, 1986, decided she would not relinquish the child to the commissioning couple. The ensuing court case, which lasted for more than a year and ended with the couple being awarded custody of the child, generated an intense debate at a time when in no US state had any regulations concerning this practice.

2   The Reuters report summing up months of investigation (Twohey 2013) found that on one Yahoo group a new ad for a child to be "rehomed" was posted once a week on average, through a transfer of guardianship requiring no more than a power of attorney and a form downloaded from the net, with the result that even people with a criminal record were able to obtain a child this way. According to US government estimates, since the late 1990s, more than twenty thousand adopted children may have been abandoned by their parents.

PART THREE

SEVEN

With Philosophy, Psychology, and Terror: Transforming Bodies into Labor Power

Within the capitalist system all methods for raising the productiveness of labour are brought about at the cost of the individual labourer; all means for the development of production transform themselves into means of domination over, and exploitation of, the producers; they mutilate the labourer into a fragment of man, degrade him to the level of appendage to the machine, destroy every remnant of charm in his work and turn it into a hated toil; they estrange from him the intellectual potentialities of the labour process in the same proportion as science is incorporated in it as an independent power; they distort the conditions under which he works, subject him during the labour process to a despotism the more hateful for its meanness; they transform his life-time into working time.

—Karl Marx, *Capital*, vol. 1, "General Law of Capitalist Accumulation"

No matter how much it proclaims its pseudo-tolerance the capitalist system in all its forms ... continues to sub-jugate all desires ... to the dictatorship of its totalitar-ian organization, founded on exploitation, property ... profit, productivity. ... Tirelessly it continues its dirty work ... suppressing, torturing and dividing up our

bodies in order to inscribe its laws on our flesh. . . .
Using every available access route into our organisms,
it insinuates into the depths of our insides its roots of
death.

—Félix Guattari, *Soft Subversions*, 1996

Our ability to resist control, or our submission to it, has
to be assessed at the level of our every move.

—Gilles Deleuze, *Negotiations*, 1995

Introduction: Why the Body?

There are different reasons why we must speak of the body
despite the vast literature that already exists on this subject.[1]
First, there is the old truth that "in the beginning is the body,"
with its desires, its powers, its manifold forms of resistance to
exploitation. As is often recognized, there is no social change,
no cultural or political innovation that is not expressed
through the body, no economic practice that is not applied to
it (Turner 1992). Second, the body is at the center of both the
main philosophical debates of our time and a cultural revolution continuing, in some respects, the project inaugurated by
the movements of the 1960s and 1970s that brought the question of instinctual liberation to the forefront of political work.
But the main reason why we must speak of the body is that
rethinking how capitalism has transformed our bodies into
labor power helps us place in a context the crisis our bodies
are currently undergoing and, at the same time, read behind
our collective and individual pathologies the search for new
anthropological paradigms.

The framework of analysis I have proposed differs from
the orthodox Marxist methodology and from the accounts
of the body and disciplinary regimes proposed by poststructuralist and postmodern theories. Unlike the orthodox
Marxist descriptions of the "formation of the proletariat,"
my analysis is not limited to changes in the body produced

by the organization of the labor process. As Marx recognized, labor power does not have an independent existence; it "exists only as a capacity in the living individual," in the living body (Marx 1976, 274). Thus, forcing people to accept the discipline of dependent labor cannot be accomplished only by "expropriating the producers from their means of subsistence" or through the compulsion that is exercised by means of the whip, the prison, and the noose. From the earliest phase of its development to the present, to force people to work at the service of others, whether the work was paid or unpaid, capitalism has had to restructure the entire process of social reproduction, remolding our relation not only to work but also to our sense of identity, to space and time, and to our social and sexual life.

The production of laboring bodies and new "disciplinary regimes" cannot therefore be purely conceived of as changes in the organization of work or as an effect of "discursive practices," as postmodern theorists propose. "Discourse production" is not a self-generating, self-subsistent activity. It is an integral part of economic and political planning and the resistances it generates. Indeed, we could write a history of the disciplines—of their paradigm shifts and innovations—from the viewpoint of the struggles that have motivated their course.

Conceiving our bodies as primarily discursive also ignores that the human body has powers, needs, desires that have developed in the course of a long process of coevolution with our natural environment and are not easily suppressed. As I have written elsewhere, this accumulated structure of needs and desires, that for thousands of years has been the precondition of our social reproduction, has been a powerful limit to the exploitation of labor, which is why capitalism, from its earliest phase of development, has struggled to domesticate our body, making it a signifier for all that is material, corporeal, finite, and opposed to "reason."

The Body in Capitalism: From the Magical Body to the Body Machine

In *Caliban and the Witch* (2004), I have argued that the "historic battle" that capitalism has waged against the body stemmed from a new political perspective positing work as the main source of accumulation, thus conceiving the body as *the condition of existence of labor power* and the main element of resistance to its expenditure. Hence the rise of "biopolitics," intended however not as a generic "management of life" but as a process that historically has required constant social, technological innovations and the destruction of all forms of life not compatible with the capitalist organization of work.

I have identified, in this context, the sixteenth- and seventeenth-century attack on magic and the contemporary rise of the mechanical philosophy as key sites for the production of a new concept of the body and the emergence of a new collaboration between philosophy and state terror. Both contributed, though with different instruments and on different registers, to produce a new conceptual and disciplinary paradigm, envisioning a body deprived of autonomous powers, fixed in space and time, capable of uniform, regular, controllable forms of behavior.

By the sixteenth century, a disciplinary machine was already set in motion that incessantly pursued the creation of an individual fit for abstract labor, yet constantly in need of being retooled, in correspondence with the changes in the organization of work, the dominant forms of technology and workers' resistance to subjugation.

Focusing on this resistance, we can see that, while in the sixteenth century the model inspiring the mechanization of the body was that of a machine moved from the outside, like the pump or the lever, by the eighteenth century, the body was already modeled on a more organic, self-moving type of machine. With the rise of *vitalism* and the theory of "instincts" (Barnes and Shapin 1979, 34), we have a new conception of the corporeal, allowing for a different type of discipline, less reliant on the whip and more dependent on the working of inner dynamisms, possibly a sign of the increasing internalization by the workforce of the disciplinary requirements of the labor process, proceeding from the consolidation of wage labor.

But the main leap that the political philosophy of the Enlightenment made in the arsenal of tools required by the transformation of the body into labor power was giving to labor discipline and to the elimination of the deviants a scientific justification. Replacing the appeal to witchcraft and devil worship, by the eighteenth century, biology and physiology were mustered to justify racial and gender hierarchies and the creation of different disciplinary regimes, in correspondence to the developing sexual and international division of labor. Much of the intellectual project of the Enlightenment rotated around this development, whether it invented race and sex (Schiebinger 2004, 143–83; Bernasconi 2011, 11–36) or it produced new monetary theories conceiving of money as a stimulus to work rather than a record of past wealth (Caffentzis 2000; Caffentzis forthcoming). Indeed, we cannot understand the culture and politics of the Enlightenment—its debates between monogenists and polygenists, its reconstruction of male/female physiology as incommensurably different (Laqueur 1990, 4–6), its craniological studies "scientifically demonstrating" the superiority of white, male brains (Stocking 1988)—unless we connect these phenomena to the naturalization of the different forms of exploitation, especially those falling outside the parameter of the wage relation.

It is tempting, in this context, to also attribute the emergence of a more organic type of mechanism, visible in the eighteenth century throughout the philosophical and scientific field, to the growing bifurcation in the workforce, and the formation of a white, male proletariat, not yet self-controlled but, as Peter Linebaugh has shown in *The London Hanged*

(1992), increasingly accepting the discipline of wage work. It is tempting, in other words, to imagine that the development of the theory of magnetism in biology, the theory of instincts in philosophy and political economy (e.g., the "instinct to trade"), and the role of electricity and gravity in physics or natural philosophy—all presupposing a more mind-like, self-propelling model of the body—reflect the growing division of labor and, accordingly, the growing differentiation in the way in which bodies were transformed into labor power. This is a hypothesis that needs to be further explored. What is certain is that with the Enlightenment we see a new step in the assimilation of the human and the machine, reconstructed views of human biology providing the ground for new mechanical conceptions of human/nature.

Psychology and the Transformation of Bodies into Labor Power in the Industrial Era

It was to be the task of psychology in the last part of the nineteenth century, to perfect the construction of the "man-machine," displacing philosophy in this strategic role. Because of its concern with psycho-physical laws and belief in causal regularities, psychology became the handmaiden of Taylorism, in charge of containing the damage done to the workers' psyche by this system and establishing appropriate connections between humans and machines. Psychology's involvement in industrial life escalated after World War I, that made a mass of uniform, obedient experimental subjects available to clinical investigation, providing a formidable laboratory for the study of "attitudes" and appropriate means of control (J.A.C. Brown 1954; Rozzi 1975, 16–17). Originally concerned with the effects of muscular work on the body, but soon called to confront workers' absenteeism and other forms of resistance to industrial discipline, as well as their resistance to its own methods and techniques, psychology soon became the discipline most directly in charge of controlling the work force. More than doctors and sociologists, psychologists have intervened in the selection of workers, conducting thousands of interviews, administering thousands of tests, to choose "the best man for the job," to spot frustrations and decide promotions (Rozzi 19).

Attributing pathologies, inherent to the industrial organization of work, to a preexisting instinctual reality (needs, drives, attitudes), and giving a mantle of scientificity to policies only dictated by the quest for profit, psychologists, since the 1930s, have been present on the factory floor, at times as permanent employees, directly intervening in the labor-capital conflict. As Renato Rozzi pointed out in *Psicologi e Operai* (1975), this intervention in the struggle has been crucial for the very development of psychology as a discipline. For the need to control workers has forced psychologists to reckon with their "subjectivity," and to adjust their own theories to the effects of workers' resistance. The struggle over the reduction of the workday, for instance, has generated a flurry of medical studies over the problem of muscular fatigue, making it, for the first time, a scientific concept (Rozzi 20n, 158).

However, industrial psychology has continued to enclose workers into a network of constraints—the discourse of drives, attitudes, instinctual dispositions—built on the systematic mystification of the origins of workers' "pathologies" and the normalization of alienated labor. Indeed, the task of the psychologist has been to negate the everyday reality of the workers, so much so that most psychological studies from this period have no value, as Rozzi points out, other than from a historical or genealogical viewpoint. It is impossible, for instance, to accept with a straight face theories such as that of "accident proneness" (Brown 257–59), which were routinely used in the 1950s in order to explain the frequency of accidents in the American workplace and affirm the uselessness of environmental improvements.

Psychology has also been essential to the reshaping of social reproduction, particularly through the rationalization of sexuality. The attention paid to Freud's construction of a biologically based conception of femininity and its relation to the turn-of-the-century crisis of the middle-class family (which he believed to be rooted in the excessive sexual repression of women) have overshadowed psychology's contribution, in the same period, to the disciplining of working-class sexuality, especially the sexuality of working-class women. Exemplary is Cesare Lombroso's theory of the prostitute as a "born criminal" (Lombroso and Ferrero [1893] 2004, 182–92), which triggered a whole production of anthropometric studies establishing that any woman who challenged her assigned female role was a throwback to a lower evolutionary stage. The construction of "homosexuality," "inversion," and masturbation as mental disorders (for example, in Kraft-Ebbing's *Psychopathia Sexualis*, 1886) and Freud's "discovery," in 1905, of the "vaginal orgasm" belong to the same project. This trend culminated with the advent of Fordism, whose epoch-making introduction of a five-dollar daily wage guaranteed to the worker the services of a wife, tying his right to sexual "satisfaction" directly to his wage, while making sex an essential part of the housewife's workload. Not accidentally, during the Great Depression, proletarian women on the dole were often kidnapped by social workers when suspected of "promiscuous behavior," for example, dating a man without any prospect of marriage, and they subsequently were placed in mental hospitals, in the hands of psychologists charged with convincing them to have their tubes tied if they wished to regain their freedom. By the 1950s, penalties for rebellious women were even more severe, with the discovery of lobotomy, a treatment that was considered especially effective for depressive, nonperforming housewives who had lost their taste for domestic work.[2]

Psychology was also brought to the colonies to theorize the existence of an African personality, justifying the inferiority of Africans to European workers and, on this basis, wage differentials and racial segregation. In South Africa, from the

1930s on, psychologists were instrumental for the application of rituals of degradation that, under the guise of "heat tolerance tests," prepared Africans to work in the gold mines, initiating them to a work situation that deprived them of any rights (Buchart 93–103).

Turning to the Present

What do we learn from this complex history today? I think we find in it three important lessons. First, we learn that the capitalist work-discipline requires the mechanization of the body, the destruction of its autonomy and creativity, and no account of our psychological and social life should ignore this reality. Second, by being complicit with the transformation of bodies into labor power, psychologists have violated the very presuppositions of their claim to science, discarding key aspects of the reality that they were expected to analyze, like workers' repulsion for the regimentation that industrial work imposes on our bodies and minds.

Most important, a history of the transformation of the body into labor power reveals the depth of the crisis that capitalism has faced since the 1960s. This is a crisis the capitalist class has tried to contain with a global reorganization of the work process but has succeeded only in relaunching the contradictions that caused it on a more explosive level. For it becomes clearer every day that the mechanisms that guarantee the discipline required for the production of value no longer operate. The movements of the 1960s and 1970s were a turning point in this respect, expressing a revolt against industrial labor that invested every articulation of the "social factory," from the assembly line to domestic labor and the gender identities functional to both. "Blue-collar blues," industrial workers' demand for "time out," rather than for more money exchanged for more work, the feminist refusal of the naturalization of reproductive labor, and the rise of the gay movement soon followed by the transsexual movement are exemplary in this context. They express a refusal to reduce one's activity to abstract labor, to renounce the satisfaction of one's desires, to relate to our bodies as machines, and a determination as well *to define our body in ways that are nondependent on our capacity to function as labor power*.

The depth of this refusal can be measured by the array of forces that have been deployed against it. The whole world economy has been restructured to contain it. From the precarization and flexibilization of work to the disinvestment by the state in the process of social reproduction—an array of policies has attempted not only to defeat these struggles, but to create a new discipline based on the ubiquity and hegemony of capitalist relations.

The institutionalization of *precarity,* for instance, has not only intensified our anxiety about survival but has also created workers who are depersonalized, adaptable, ready at any moment to change occupation (Berardi 2009a; 2009b). Our loss of identity and powerlessness is further intensified by the computerization and automation of work that promote highly mechanical, militaristic, dehumanizing types of behavior, in which the person is reduced to just a component of a broader mechanical system (Levidow and Robins 1989). Indeed, the abstraction and regimentation of labor has reached today its completion and so has our sense of alienation and desocialization. What levels of stress this situation is producing in our lives can be measured by the massification of mental illness—panic, anxiety, fear, attention deficit—and the escalating consumption of drugs from Prozac to Viagra. It has also been argued that the success of "reality TV" shows is a product of this psychological sense of estrangement from our lives. For the desire to see how others live, what they do, and compare ourselves to them—which, as Renata Salecl (2004) has shown, drives this branch of industry—reveals a sense that our life is being lost, though the same programs lead to more virtuality rather than a better hold on reality.

Fear and anxiety caused by the uncertainty of survival are only one aspect of the terror that today is strategically employed to suffocate the revolt against the global work-machine. Equally important is the militarization of everyday life, now an international trend. This begins with the policy of mass incarceration adopted in the 1990s in the United States, which can be read as a war waged especially against black youth, and the proliferation of detention centers for immigrants throughout the European Community. We have also seen an escalation in the harshness of punishment, like mandatory sentencing, "three-strikes" laws, the use of tasers, and solitary confinement, and the increase in the number of women and children arrested (Williams 2006, 205; Solinger et al. 2010; Donner 2000). Torture is now routinely practiced not only in the "war on terror" but also in US prisons. As Kristian Williams suggests (2006), these are neither anomalies nor unintended effects of a derailing of justice. The militarization of everyday life punishes protest, checks the escape from the nets of economic restructuring, and maintains a racialized division of labor, asserting the right of the state to destroy the body of the citizen (216). Indeed, today's prison system does not pretend to have a reforming affect, functioning unambiguously as an instrument of terror and class rule.

This massive deployment of force is what so far has contained the revolt against capitalist organization of work. But as capital's inability to satisfy our most basic needs becomes more and more evident, the transformation of our bodies into labor power becomes every day more problematic. The very instruments of terror are breaking down. Witness the increasing refusal of war and soldiering, revealed by the high number of suicides in the now-voluntary US Army, which has triggered a massive reeducation and "fitness" program. As for the institutionalization of precarity, this is a double-edged weapon, for it sets the conditions for a radical denaturalization of dependent work and the loss of the very skills that sociologists have long considered indispensable in an industrial population. As Chris Carlsson has documented in his *Nowtopia* (2008), more people are seeking alternatives to a life regulated by work and the market both because, in a precarized labor regime, work can no longer be a source of identity formation, and because they wish to be more creative. Along the same lines, workers' struggles today exhibit patterns different from the traditional strike, reflecting a search for new models of humanity and new relations between human beings and nature. We see it in the interest for the discourse and practice of the "commons," which is already spawning many new initiatives, like time banks, barter exchanges, urban gardens, and community-based accountability structures. We see it also in the preference for *androgynous* models of gender identity, the rise of the transsexual and intersex movements, and the queer rejection of gender, with all its implications expressing a questioning of the sexual division of labor. I must also mention the globally spreading passion for tattoos and the art of body decoration, which is creating new and imagined communities across sex, race, and class boundaries. All these phenomena point not only to a breakdown of disciplinary mechanisms but also to a desire for a remolding of our humanity in ways very different from, in fact opposite to, those that centuries of capitalist discipline have imposed on us.

Where will psychologists position themselves with respect to these phenomena? This, today, is an open question. Psychology had demonstrated itself able to transform itself and recognize the subjectivity of the subjects it studies. But it has not found the courage to break with Power. Despite the radical critique to which it was subjected in the 1960s by dissident psychologists and psychiatrists (like Félix Guattari and Franco Basaglia), mainstream psychology remains an accomplice of power. Psychologists today in the United States are actively engaged in the selection of torture techniques and interrogation methods. Unlike the American Psychiatric Association, the American Psychological Association has so far refused to implement a resolution passed by its members barring them from participating in interrogation at sites where international law or the Geneva Convention are violated.

Psychologists are to blame not only for their actions, but also or their omissions. With few exceptions, they have not criticized as pathogenic the capitalist organization and discipline of work and have instead accepted the sale of labor as a normal fact of social life, interpreting the revolt against it as an abnormality to be suffocated in a discourse about fixed predispositions. A simple but telling example of this omission is the absence of any psychological investigation into the significance and value of wage rates and particularly pay raises or pay cuts as (de)motivating factors. "Although there is a voluminous psychological literature on performance evaluation, little of this research examines the consequences of linking pay to evaluated performance in work setting" (Rynes, Gerhart, and Parks-Leduc 2005, 572–73). Similarly, there is no recognition that mental disorders may be caused by such economic factors as unemployment, lack of health insurance, and rebellion against work. Instead, psychologists have followed economists in conducting "happiness studies," in a renewed effort to convince us that positive thinking, optimism, and above all "resilience"—the new catchword in the sky of semantic disciplinary tools—are the keys to success. It can be noted here that the doyen of "happiness studies," Martin Seligman, has lectured to the US Army and the CIA on the state of "learned helplessness" that presumably develops as part of the torture process, receiving from the army a $31 million grant to train soldiers to become more "resilient" to the traumas provoked by war (Greenberg 2010, 34).

The time has come for psychologists to denounce the techniques devised to transform the body into labor power, which inevitably leads from philosophy to terror and from psychology to torture. Psychology can no longer displace the pathologies provoked by capitalism onto a preconstituted human nature or continue to produce straitjackets into which to force our bodies while ignoring the daily violation of their integrity at the hand of the economic and political system in which we live.

Notes

1 An early version of this article was presented at the Conference on Theoretical Psychology held in Thessaloniki on June 28, 2011.

2 Lobotomy was a mainstream procedure for more than two decades. Most lobotomy procedures were done in the United States, where by the 1950s approximately forty thousand people were lobotomized, the first being performed in 1936. The peak year was 1949, when more than five thousand procedures were undertaken. Lobotomies were performed also in Great Britain and the three Nordic countries of Finland, Norway, and Sweden. Scandinavian hospitals lobotomized 2.5 times as many people per capita as hospitals in the US. The overwhelming majority of lobotomy patients were women. See Joel Braslow, "Therapeutic Effectiveness and Social Context: The Case of Lobotomy in a California State Hospital, 1947–1954," *Western Journal of Medicine* 170, no. 5 (June 1999): 293–96. Despite their loss of spontaneity and individual desires, both doctors and husband believed lobotomized women greatly benefited from the operations, considering their her ability to cook, clean, and do housework an integral part of their recovery.

EIGHT

Origins and Development of Sexual Work in the United States and Britain

From the beginning of capitalist society, sexual work has performed two fundamental functions in the context of capitalist production and the capitalist division of labor. On one side, it has ensured the procreation of new workers. On the other, it has been a key aspect of their daily reproduction, as sexual release has been, for men at least, the safety valve for the tensions accumulated during the workday, all the more indispensable as for a long time sex was one of the few pleasures conceded to them. The very concept of the "proletariat" signified a working class that reproduced itself prolifically not only because one more child meant another factory hand and another pay but also because sex was the only pleasure of the poor.

Despite its importance, during the first phase of industrialization, the sexual activity of the working class was not subjected to much state regulation. In this phase, which lasted until the second half of the nineteenth century, the main concern of the capitalist class was the quantity rather than the quality of the labor power to be produced. That the English workers, male and female, died on average at about thirty-five years of age did not matter to the British factory owners, as long as those years were all spent in a factory, from sunup to sundown, from the first years of life until death, and as long as new labor power was abundantly procreated to replace those continually eliminated.[1] English workers, male and female, were only expected to produce an abundant prole, and little consideration was given to their "moral conduct." Indeed, it was expected that promiscuousness would be a norm in the slum dormitories where, in Glasgow as in New York, workers spent the few hours they had away from the factory. It was also expected that English and American female workers would alternate or integrate factory work with prostitution, which exploded in these countries in conjunction with the takeoff of the industrialization process.[2]

It was in the second half of the nineteenth century that things started to change, as, under the pressure of working-class struggle, a restructuring of production took place that demanded a different type of worker and, accordingly, a change in the process of its reproduction. It was the shift from light industry to heavy industry, from the mechanical frame to the steam engine, from the production of cloth to that of coal and steel, that created the need for a worker less emaciated, less prone to disease, more capable of sustaining the intense rhythms of work that the shift to heavy industry required. It is in this context that the capitalist class, generally indifferent to the high mortality rates of the industrial workers, crafted a new reproduction strategy, increasing the male wage, returning proletarian women to the home and, at the same time, increasing the intensity of factory work, which the better-reproduced waged worker would now be capable to perform.

Thus, hand in hand with introduction of Taylorism and a new regimentation of the work process, in the second part of the nineteenth century, we have a reform of the working-class family centered on the construction of a new domestic role for the woman that would make of her the guarantor of the production of a more qualified workforce. This meant enticing women to not only procreate to fill the ranks of the workforce but to guarantee the daily reproduction of the laborers, through the provision of the physical, emotional, and sexual services necessary to reintegrate their capacity to work.

As mentioned, the reorganization of work that took place in England between 1850 and 1880 was dictated by the need to secure a healthier, more disciplined, and more productive labor force and, above all, break the surge of working-class organization. A further consideration, however, was the realization that the recruitment of women into the factories had destroyed their acceptance of and capacity for reproductive work to such an extent that if remedies were not found, the reproduction of the English working class would be severely jeopardized. Suffice to read the reports periodically drafted by government appointed factory inspectors in England, between 1840 and 1880, on the conduct of the female factory hands to realize that more was at stake, in the advocated change of reproductive regime, than concern for the health and combativeness of the male part of the working class.

Undisciplined, indifferent to housework, family, and morality, determined to have a good time in the few hours free from work available to them, ready to leave the home for the street, the bar, where they would drink and smoke like men, alienated from their children, married or unmarried female factory hands, in the bourgeois imagination, were a threat to the production of a stable labor force and had to be domesticated. It was in this context that the "domestication" of the working-class family and the creation the full-time working-class housewife became a state policy, also inaugurating a new form of capital accumulation.

As if suddenly awakened to the reality of factory life, by the 1850s a host of reformers began to thunder against the long hours women spent away from the home, and by means of "protective legislation" first eliminated female night shifts and later ousted married women from the factories, so that they could be reeducated to function like the "angels of the hearth," cognizant of the arts of patience and subordination, especially since the work to which they were destined was not to be paid.

The idealization of "female virtue," until the turn of the century reserved for the women of the middle and upper class, was thus extended to working-class women to hide the unpaid labor expected of them. Not surprisingly, we see in this period a new ideological campaign promoting among the working class the ideals of *maternity* and *love*, understood as the capacity for absolute self-sacrifice. Fantine, the prostitute mother of *Les Misérables*, who sells her hair and two of her teeth to support her infant child, was a proper embodiment of this ideal. "Conjugal love" and "motherly instinct" are themes that permeate the discourse of Victorian reformers, together with complaints about the pernicious effects of factory work on women's morality and reproductive role.

Regulating housework would not be possible, however, without regulating sexual work. As with housework, what characterized the sexual politics of capital and the state in this phase was the extension to the proletarian woman of the principles already regulating the sexual conduct of women in the bourgeois family. First among them was the negation of female sexuality as a source of pleasure and monetary gain for women. For the transformation of the female factory-worker-prostitute—in both cases a paid worker—into an unpaid mother-wife ready to sacrifice her own interest and desire for the well-being of her family, an essential premise was the "purification" of the maternal role from any erotic element.

This meant that the wife-mother should only enjoy the pleasure of "love," conceived as a sentiment free from any desire for sex and remuneration. In sexual work itself, the division of labor between "sex for procreation" and "sex for pleasure," and, in the case of women, the association of sex with antisocial characteristics, was deepened. Both in the US and England, a new regulation of prostitution was introduced aiming to separate "honest women" from "prostitutes"—a distinction which the recruitment of women into factory work had dissipated. William Acton, one of the promoters of the reform in England, noted how pernicious was the constant presence of prostitutes in public places. The reasons he offered speak volumes:

> My chief interest lay in considering the effect produced upon married women by becoming accustomed at these *réunions* to witness the vicious and profligate sister-hood flaunting it gaily, or "first rate" in their language, accepting all the attentions of men, freely plied with liquor, sitting in the best places, dressed far above their station, with plenty of money to spend, denying them-selves no amusements or enjoyment, encumbered with no domestic duties, and burdened with no children. Whatever the purport of the drama might have been, this actual superiority of a loose life could not have escaped the attention of the quick-witted sex. (Acton [1857] 1969, 54–55).

Acton's initiative was also prompted by another concern: the spread of venereal diseases, syphilis in particular, among the proletariat:

> The reader who is a conscientious parent must perforce support me; for, were the sanitary measures I advocate in operation, with what diminished anxiety would he not contemplate the progress of his boys from infancy to manhood? The statesman and the political econo-mists are mine already, for are not armies and navies invalidated—is not labour enfeebled—is not even popu-lation deteriorated by the evils against which I propose we should contend? (Acton [1857] 1969, 27).

Regulating prostitution meant subjecting sex workers to medical control, according to the model adopted in France since the first half of the nineteenth century.

With this regulation, that made the state, through the police and the medical profession, the direct supervisor of sex work, we have *the institutionalization of the prostitute and the mother as separate, mutually exclusive female figures and functions, that is, the institutionalization of a maternity without pleasure and a "pleasure" without maternity.* Social policy began to require that the prostitute must not become a mother.[3] Her maternity had to be hidden, removed from the place of her work. In the literature of the time, the child of the prostitute lives in the countryside, consigned to charitable caretakers. By contrast, the mother, the spouse, the "honest woman" would be expected to look at sex only as a domestic service, a conjugal duty that she could not escape, but that would give her no pleasure. The only sex conceded to the mother would be the sex made clean by marriage and procreation—that is, by endless hours of unpaid labor, consumed with little joy, and always accompanied by the fear of impregnation. Hence, the classic image, handed down to us from nineteenth-century novels, of the woman suffering the advances of her husband, careful not to contradict the aura of sanctity by which society wanted to encircle her head.

The division of the labors of sex work and mothering, however, has been possible only because capital has used much psychological and physical violence to impose it. The destiny of the unwed mother, the "seduced and abandoned" that, together with the exaltation of motherly sacrifices, filled the pages of nineteenth-century literature, has been a constant warning to women that everything was preferable to "losing one's honor" and being considered a "slut." But the whip that most has served to keep women in place has been the condition in which the prostitute, at the proletarian level, has been forced to live, as she increasingly was isolated from other women and subjected to constant state control.

But despite the criminalization of prostitution, efforts to create a respectable working-class family were for a long time frustrated. For only a small part of the male working class could benefit from the kind of wages that would enable a family to survive purely on "his job," and sex work was always for proletarian women the most readily available form of income, and the one to which they were forced by the volatility of sexual affairs, that often left them with children to support alone. It was a sobering discovery, in the 1970s, to learn that in Italy, before World War I, most proletarian children at birth had been registered as fathered by "NN" (*nomen nescio*, name unknown). Employers took advantage of the poverty of women to force them into prostitution, to keep what jobs they may have or to prevent their husbands from being laid off.

As for the "honest" working-class women, they have always known that the dividing line between marriage and prostitution, between the whore and the respectable woman, has been very thin. Proletarian women have always known that for women marriage meant being "a servant by the day and a whore at night,"[4] for every time they planned to abandon the conjugal bed, they had to reckon with their financial poverty. Still, the construction of female sexuality as a service, and its negation as pleasure, have for a long time kept alive the idea that female sexuality is sinful and redeemable only through marriage and procreation, and it has produced a situation where *every woman was considered a potential prostitute* to be constantly controlled. As a result, generations of women, before the rise of the feminist movement, have lived their sexuality as something shameful and have had to prove that they were not prostitutes. At the same time, prostitution, though an object of social condemnation to be controlled by the state, has been recognized as a necessary component of the reproduction of labor power, precisely because it has been assumed that the wife would not be able to completely satisfy her husband's sexual needs.

This explains why *sexual work was the first aspect of housework that was socialized*. The state brothel, the "casa chiusa" (closed house) or "maison des femmes," typical of the first phase of capital's planning of sexual work, *has institutionalized the woman as a collective lover, working directly or indirectly at the service of the state as the collective husband and pimp.* Besides ghettoizing women, who would be paid to perform what millions provided for free, the socialization of sexual work has responded to criteria of productive efficiency. The *Taylorization of coitus*, typical of the brothel, has greatly increased the productivity of sexual work. Low-cost, easily accessible, state-sponsored sex was the ideal for a worker who, after spending a day in a factory or an office, would not have the time and energy to look for amorous adventures or embark on the path of voluntary relations.

The Struggle against Sexual Work

With the rise of the nuclear family and marital sex a new phase in the history of women's struggle against housework and sexual work began. Evidence of this struggle is the rise of divorce, at the turn of the twentieth century, above all in the US and England, and in the middle class, where the nuclear family model was first adopted.

As O'Neill (1967) points out, "Until about the middle of the nineteenth century divorces were a rare events in the Western world; thereafter they occurred at such a steadily increasing rate that by the end of the century the legal dissolution of marriage was recognized as a major social phenomenon" (O'Neill 1). He continues: "If we consider the Victorian family as a new institution . . . we can see why divorce became a necessary part of the family system. When the family becomes the center of social organization, its intimacy becomes suffocating, its constraints unbearable and its expectations too high to be realized" (6).

O'Neill and his contemporaries were well aware that behind the family crisis and the rush to divorce there was the rebellion of women. In the US the bulk of the requests for divorce were presented by women. Divorce was not the only way in which women expressed their refusal of family discipline. In this same period, both in the US and England, the fertility rate began to fall. From 1850 to 1900, the family in the US shrank by one member. Simultaneously, in both countries, a feminist movement developed, inspired by the slave abolitionist movement, that took "domestic slavery" as its target.

"Are Women to Blame?," the title of a symposium on divorce, published by the *North American Review* in 1889, was a typical example of the attack launched against women in this period. Women were accused of being greedy or selfish, of expecting too much from marriage, of having a weak sense of responsibility, and of subordinating the common well-being to their narrow personal interest. Even when they did not divorce, women carried on a daily struggle against housework and sexual work, often taking the form of illness and desexualization. Already in 1854, Mary Nichols, an American doctor and promoter of family reform, would write:

> Nine tenths of the children born are not desired by the mother. . . . A vast number of the women of civilization have neither the sexual nor maternal passion. All women want love and support. They do not want to bear children or to be harlots for this love or this support. In marriage as it at present exists the instinct against bearing children and against submitting to amative embrace, is almost as general as the love for children after they are born. The obliteration of the maternal and sexual instinct in woman is a terrible pathological fact (quoted in Cott 286).

Women used the excuse of feebleness, fragility, and sudden illnesses (migraines, fainting, hysteria) to avoid conjugal duties and the danger of unwanted pregnancies. That these were not, properly speaking, "illnesses" but forms of resistance to housework and sexual work is demonstrated not only by the pervasive character of this phenomena, but also by the complaints of the husbands and the sermons of the doctors. This is how an American doctor, Mrs. R.B. Gleason, described the dialectics of illness and refusal, viewed both from a woman's and a man's viewpoint in the turn-of-the-century middle-class family:

> I ought never to have been married, for my life is one prolonged agony. I could endure it myself alone, but the thought that I am, from year to year, becoming the mother of those who are to partake of and perpetuate the misery that I endure, makes me so wretched that I am well-nigh distracted (Cott 274).

Says the doctor:

> The prospective husband may take great care to protect the fair but frail one of his choice; he may . . . fondly cherish the wife of his youth when she aches constantly and ages prematurely; still he has no helpmate—no one to double life's joys or lighten life's labors for him. Some sick women grow selfish and forget that, in a partnership such as theirs, others suffer when they suffer. Every true husband has but half a life who has a sick wife (274).

Says the husband:

> Can she ever be well? (275)

When they did not fall ill, women became frigid or, in Mary Nichols's words, they inherited "an apathetic state that does not impel them to any material union" (Cott 286). In the context of a sexual discipline that denied women, especially in the middle class, control over their sexual life, frigidity and the proliferation of bodily aches were effective forms of refusal that could be masked as an extension of the normal defense of chastity, that is, as an excess of virtue that allowed women to turn the tables to their advantage and present themselves as the true defenders of sexual morality. In this way, middle-class Victorian women were often able to refuse their sexual duties more than their granddaughters would be able to do. For after decades of women's refusal of sexual work, psychologists, sociologists, and other "experts" have wised up and are now less ready to retreat. Today, in fact, a whole campaign is mounted that guilt-trips the "frigid woman," not least with the charge of not being liberated.

The blossoming of the social sciences in the nineteenth century must in part be connected to the crisis of the family and women's refusal of it. Psychoanalysis was born as the science of sexual control, charged with providing strategies for the reform of family relations. In both the US and England, plans for the reformation of sexuality emerge in the first decade of the twentieth century. Books, booklets, pamphlets, essays, and treatises were devoted to the family and the "divorce problem," revealing not only the depth of the crisis but also the growing awareness that a new sexual/family ethics would be needed. Thus, while in the US the more conservative circles founded the League for the Protection of the Family and radical women advocated free unions and argued that for this system to work "it would be necessary for the state to subsidize all mothers as a matter of right" (O'Neill 104), sociologists and psychologists joined the debate, proposing that the problem be scientifically resolved. It would be Freud's task to systematize the new sexual code, which is why Freud's work became so popular in both countries.

Freud and the Reform of Sexual Work

On the surface, Freud's theory seems to concern sexuality in general, but its real target was female sexuality. Freud's work was a response to women's refusals of housework, procreation, and sexual work. As his writings well indicate, he was deeply aware that the "family crisis" stemmed from the fact that women did not want to or could not do their job. He was also concerned for the growth of male impotence, which had assumed such proportions as to be described by him as one of the main social phenomena of his time. Freud attributed the latter to the "extension of the demands made upon women onto the sexual life of the male, and the taboo on sexual intercourse except in monogamous marriage." He wrote: "Civilized sexual morality ... by glorifying monogamy ... cripples virile selection—the sole influence by which an improvement of the race can be obtained" (Freud 1972, 11).

The struggle of women against sexual work not only jeopardized their role as domestic lovers and produced disaffected males; it also put at risk their role (perhaps more important at the time) as procreators. "I do not know," he wrote, "if the anaesthetic type of women is also found outside of civilized education, but I consider it probable. In any case, these women who conceive without pleasure show later little willingness to endure frequent childbirths, accompanied as they are by pain, so that the training that precedes marriage directly frustrates the very aim of marriage" (25).

Freud's strategy was to (re)integrate sex into the domestic workday and discipline, in order to reconstruct on more solid bases, by means of a freer and satisfying sexual life, the woman's traditional role of wife and mother. In other words, with Freud *sexuality is placed at the service of the consolidation of housework* and is turned into an element of work, soon to become itself a duty. Freud's prescription is a freer sexuality for a healthier family life, for a family in which the woman would identify with her wifely function, instead of becoming hysterical, neurotic, and wrapping herself into a sheet of frigidity after the first months of marriage and perhaps being tempted to transgress through "degenerate" experiences such as lesbianism.

Beginning with Freud, sexual liberation for women has meant an intensification of domestic work. The model of the wife and mother cultivated by the psychology profession was no longer that of the mother-procreator of an abundant off-spring but that of the wife-lover who had to guarantee higher levels of pleasure to her husband than what was obtainable from the simple penetration of a passive or resistant body.

In the United States, the reintegration of sexuality into housework began to take hold in the proletarian family with the development of domesticity in the Progressive Era and it accelerated with the Fordist reorganization of work and wages. It came with the assembly line, the five-dollar-a-day wage and the work speed-up, which demanded that the men rest at night instead of prowling around in the saloons, so as to be fresh and restored for another day of hard work. The stiff work-discipline and speed-up that Taylorism and Fordism introduced in the American factory required a new hygiene, a new sexual regime, and therefore the reconversion of sexuality and family life. In other words, for the workers to be able to sustain the regimentation of factory life, the wage had to buy a more substantial sexuality than that provided by the casual encounters in the saloons. Making the home more attractive, through the reorganization of home-based sexual work, was also vital at a time of raising wages, which could otherwise be spent on merrymaking.

The shift was also prompted by political considerations. The attempt to win men over to the home and away from the saloon, which intensified after World War I, was prompted by the saloon having been a center for political organizing and debate as well as for prostitution.

For the housewife this reorganization meant that she would have to continue to make children and would have to worry that her hips might become too large, and here began the array of diets. She would continue washing dishes and floors but with polished nails and frills on her apron, and she would continue to slave from sunup to sundown but would have to spruce herself up to adequately greet her husband's return. At this point, saying no in bed became more difficult. In fact, new canons, publicized by psychology books and women's journals, began to stress that the sexual union was crucial for a well-functioning marriage.

Starting in the in the 1950s there was also a change in the function of prostitution. As the century progressed, the average American male less and less resorted to prostitution for the satisfaction of his needs. What saved the family, however, more than anything else, was the limited access that women had to wages of their own. But all was not well within the American family, as seen in the high number of divorces in the postwar period (both in England and the United States). The more was asked of women and the family, the more women's refusal grew, which could not yet be a refusal of marriage, for obvious economic reasons, but was rather *a demand for higher mobility within marriage*—that is a demand for the possibility of moving from husband to husband (as from employer to employer) and exacting better conditions of housework. In this period, the struggle for the second job (and for welfare) became closely connected with the struggle against the family, as the factory or the office often represented for women the only alternative to unpaid housework, to their isolation within the family, and to subordination to their husbands' desires. Not accidentally, men for a long time saw women's second job as the antechamber to prostitution. Until the explosion of the welfare struggle, having an outside job was often the only way for women to get out of the house, to meet people, to escape an insufferable marriage.

But already at the beginning of the 1950s, the Kinsey Report rang an alarm bell, as it demonstrated women's resistance to expending adequate levels of sexual work. It was discovered that many American women were frigid, that they did not participate in their sex work but only went through the motions. It was also discovered that half of American males had or wanted to have homosexual relations. Similar conclusions were reached by an investigation on marriage in the

American working class conducted a few years later. Here too it was found that a quarter of married women made love only as a pure conjugal duty and an extremely high number of them did not derive any pleasure from it (Komarovsky [1967], 83). It was at this point that capital in the US launched a massive campaign on the sexual front, determined to defeat with the arms of theory and practice the obstinate apathy of so many women toward sexuality. The dominant theme in this campaign was the quest for female orgasm, increasingly taken as the test of perfection in the conjugal union. Female orgasm, in the 1960s, became the motif of a whole series of psychological studies, culminating with Masters and Johnson's alleged epochal discovery that not only did female orgasm exist but also in a multiple form.

With the Masters and Johnson experiments, the productivity required of women's sexual work was fixed at very high quotas. Not only could women make love and reach orgasm, *they had to*. If we did not succeed, we were not real women; even worse, we were not "liberated." This message was communicated to us in the 1960s from movie screens, the pages of women's journals, and the "do-it-yourself" handbooks that taught us the positions enabling us to reach a satisfactory copulation. It was also preached by psychoanalysts who established that a "full" sexual relation is a condition for social and psychological balance. By the 1970s "sex clinics" and "sex shops" began to appear, and family life underwent a remarkable restructuring, with the legitimization of premarital and extramarital relations, "open marriage," group sex, and the acceptance of autoeroticism. Meanwhile, just to be safe, technological innovation produced the vibrator for those women who even the latest updating of the Kama Sutra could not put to work.

What Has This Meant for Women?

Let us state it in no uncertain terms. For the women of today no less than for our mothers and grandmothers, sexual liberation can only mean liberation from "sex," rather than intensification of sexual work.

"Liberation from sex" means liberation from the conditions in which we are forced to live our sexuality, which transform this activity into an arduous work, full of incognita and accidents, not least the danger of remaining pregnant, given that even the latest contraceptives are taken at a considerable health risk. Until these conditions prevail, any "progress" brings more work and anxieties. Undoubtedly, it is a great advantage not to be lynched by fathers, brothers, and husbands if it is discovered that we are not virgins or that we are "unfaithful" and "misbehave"—although, the number of women murdered by their partners because they wish to leave them is constantly growing. But sexuality continues to be for us a source of anxiety, for "sexual liberation" has been turned into a duty that we must accept if we do not want to be accused of being backward. Thus, while our grandmothers, after a day of hard work, could go to sleep in peace with the excuse of a migraine, we, their liberated granddaughters, feel guilty when refusing to have sex, not actively participating in it, or even when not enjoying it.

To come, to have an orgasm, has become such a categorical imperative, that we feel uneasy to admit that "nothing is happening," and to men's insistent questions we respond with a lie or force ourselves to make another effort, with the result that often our beds feel like a gym.

But the main difference is that our mothers and grandmothers looked at sexual services within a logic of exchange: you went to bed with the man you married, that is, the man who promised you a certain financial security. Today, instead, we work for free, in bed as in the kitchen, not only because sexual work is unpaid but because increasingly we provide sexual services without expecting anything in return. Indeed, the symbol of the liberated woman is the woman who is always available but in return does not ask anything any longer.

Notes

1   It is significant, for instance, that in the US, throughout the nine-teenth century, the age of consent for females was set at about ten.

2   It is generally recognized that low female wages and the promiscu-ous mixing of the sexes in the slums were the main causes of the "explosion" of prostitution that took place in England in the first phase of the industrialization process. As William Acton wrote in his famous work on prostitution: "Many women . . . swell the ranks of prostitution through being by their position particularly exposed to temptation. The women to whom this remark applies are chiefly actresses, milliners, shop-girls, domestic servants and women employed in factories or working in agricultural gangs. . . . It is a shameful fact, but nonetheless true, that the lowness of the wage paid to the work-women in various trades is a fruitful source of prostitution" (Acton [1857] 1969, 129–30). Not surprisingly, for a long time, in the bourgeois family, the promiscuous or "immoral" conduct of women was punished as a form of *déclassement*. "To behave like one of those women" meant to behave like proletarian women, the women of the "lower classes."

3   This, however, was not an easy task. Significantly, Acton lamented:

> Prostitutes do not, as is generally supposed, die in harness . . . on the contrary, they, for the most part, become, sooner or later, with tarnished bodies and polluted minds, wives and mothers, while among some classes of the people the moral sentiment is so depraved that the woman who lives by the hire of her person is received on almost equal terms to social inter-course. It is clear, then, that though we may call these women outcasts and pariahs, they have a powerful influence for evil on all ranks of the community. The moral injury inflicted on society by prostitution is incalculable; the physical injury is at least as great. (Acton [1857] 1969, 84–85).

4   This is how the grandmother of a feminist friend described her life.

NINE

Mormons in Space Revisited
with George Caffentzis

How to explain capital's urge to leave the earth? To simultaneously destroy it and transcend it? Why all this dreaming of space shuttles, space colonies, travels to Mars, mixed with the militarization of space? Does capitalism want to destroy this messy earth as it wants to rewire our bodies? Is this capitalism's nasty secret: the final destruction of the earth and of our recalcitrant bodies—both residues of a billion years of noncapitalist formation? Why the simultaneous attempt to militarize space and recode the chromosomes and our neural system? Why, if not to define a truly capitalist being, in a purely capitalist plasm and a purely capitalist sequence of work events—weightless, formless neurosystems ready for infinite rewebbing?

"Outer space" is not space as we know it. Capital lusts for it not because of the minerals that can be found or produced on Mars, but for what they can do to us when they get us there.

If one tried to define the spirit of our time—breathing through the New Right—one would be confronted with an undecipherable puzzle. On the one side, these are the spokesmen for a scientific and technological revolution that a few years ago would have smacked of science fiction: gene splicing, recombinant DNA, time compression techniques, space colonies. At the same time, the circles of the New Right have witnessed a revival of religious tendencies and moral conservatism that one would have thought buried once and for all with the Puritan Founding Fathers. Wherever you turn, God-fearing, Satan-minded groups are sprawling like mushrooms: Christian Voice, Pro-Family Forum, National Prayer Campaign, Eagle Forum, Right to Life Commission, Fund to Restore an Educated Electorate, Institute for Christian Economics. Seen in its general contours, then, the body of the New Right seems stretching in two opposite directions, attempting at once a bold leap into the past and an equally bold leap into the future.

The puzzle increases when we realize that these are not separate sects, but in more than one way they involve the same people and the same money. Despite a few petty squabbles and a few contortions to keep up the pluralism facade, the hand that sends the shuttle into orbit or recombines mice and rabbits is the same that pushes gays, trans people, and women who abort to the stake and draws a big cross not just through the twentieth century but the nineteenth and eighteenth as well.

To what extent the right-to-life apostles and the science futurologists are one soul, one mission, is best seen, if not in the lives of their individual spokesmen then in the harmony of intent they display when confronted with the "key issues" of the time. When it comes to economic and political matters, all shreds of difference drop off and both souls of the New Right pull money and resources toward common goals. Free-market, laissez-faire economics, the militarization of the country (what is called "building a strong military defense"), bolstering "internal security," for example, giving the FBI and CIA free rein to police our daily life, cutting all social spending except that devoted to building prisons and ensuring that millions will fill them; in a word, asserting US capital's ownership of the world and setting "America" to work at the minimum wage (or below) are goals for which all the New Right swears on the Bible.

A clue to understanding the double soul of the New Right is to realize that its mixture of reactionary social policies and scientific boldness is not a novelty in the history of capitalism. If we look at the beginning of capitalism—the sixteenth and seventeenth centuries to which the Moral Majority would happily return—we see a similar situation in the countries that witnessed the capitalist "takeoff." At the time when Galileo was pointing his telescope to the moon and Francis Bacon was laying the foundations of scientific rationality, women and gays were burned on the stake throughout Europe, with the universal blessing of the modernizing European intelligentsia.

A sudden craze? An inexplicable fall into barbarism? In reality, the witch hunt was part and parcel of that attempt at "human perfectibility" that is commonly acknowledged as the dream of the fathers of modern rationalism. For the thrust of the emerging capitalist class toward the domination and exploitation of nature would have remained a dead letter without the concomitant creation of a new type of individual whose behavior would be as regular, predictable, and controllable as that of the newly discovered natural laws. To achieve this purpose one had to destroy that magical conception of the world that made indigenous people in the colonies believe that it was a sacrilege to mine the earth, and taught people in Europe that on "unlucky days" all enterprise should be avoided. The witch hunt, moreover, gave the state control over the main source of labor, the woman's body, by criminalizing abortion and all forms of contraception as a crime against humanity. On the stake died the adulteress, the woman of ill repute, the lesbian, the woman who lived alone or lacked maternal spirit or had illegitimate children. On the stake ended many beggars, who had launched their curses against those refusing them some ale and bread. The fathers of modern rationalism approved. Some even complained that the state did not go far enough. Notoriously, Jean Bodin insisted that witches should not be "mercifully" strangled before being given to the flames.

That today we find a similar situation prevailing in the US is a sign of capital's crisis. Always, when uncertain of its foundations, capital goes down to basics. At present, this means attempting a bold technological leap which, on one side (at the production pole), concentrates capital and automates work to an unprecedented degree and, on the other, consigns millions of workers either to wagelesness, unemployment, or intensive labor, paid at minimum rates, on the model of the much acclaimed "free enterprise zones." This involves a reorganization of the process whereby labor is reproduced.

The institutionalization of repression and self-discipline along the line of the New Christian Right is required today at both ends of the working-class spectrum: for those destined to temporary, low-waged jobs, or to a perennial quest for employment, as well as for those destined to work with the most sophisticated equipment technology can produce. Let's not be mistaken. From Wall Street to the army, all capital's utopias are predicated on an infinitesimal micropolitics at the level of the body, curbing our animal spirits and refining the meaning of the "pursuit of happiness." This is especially necessary for the development of the high-tech workers who, unlike those at the lower echelons of the working class, cannot be run by the stick, as the machines they work with are infinitely more costly.

What the launching of high-tech industry needs most today is a technological leap in the human machine—a big evolutionary step creating a new type of worker to match capital's investment needs. What are the faculties required by the new being that our futurologists advocate? A look at the debate on space colonies is revealing. All agree that the main impediment to the development of human colonies in space is biosocial rather than technological. You may glue the space shuttle's tiles together tightly enough to launch them into Mars, but producing the right space worker is a problem that even the genetic breakthroughs have not resolved. An individual is needed who can endure social isolation and sensory deprivation for long periods of time without breaking down, perform "perfectly" in an extremely hostile/alien and artificial environment and

under enormous stress, achieve a superb control of psychological reactions (anger, hate, indecisiveness) and bodily functions (consider that it takes one hour just to shit in space!).

Our all-too-human frailties can be disastrous in the
fragile world of life in space. This requires total obedience,
conformity, and receptivity to commands. There can be little
tolerance for deviations and disagreements when the most
minute act of sabotage can have catastrophic consequences
for the costly, complex, and powerful equipment entrusted
in people's hands. Not only must the space technicians have
a quasi-religious relation to their machines; they themselves
must become more and more machine-like, achieving a perfect
symbiosis with computers which, in the long nights of space,
are often their only and most reliable guide, their companions,
their buddies, their friends.

Space workers, then, must be ascetic types, pure in body
and soul, perfect in their performance, obedient like well-
wound clocks and extremely fetishistic in their mental modes.
Where can these gems be bred? In a fundamentalist religious
sect. To put it in the words of biologist Garrett Hardin:

> What group would be most suitable to this most recent
> Brave New World (the space colony)? Probably a reli-
> gious group. There must be unity of thought and the
> acceptance of discipline. But the colonists couldn't be
> a bunch of Unitarians or Quakers, for these people
> regard the individual conscience as the best guide to
> action. Space colonies' existence would require some-
> thing more like the Hutterites or the Mormons for its
> inhabitants. . . . Integration could not be risked on this
> delicate vessel, for fear of sabotage and terrorism. Only
> "purification" would do (Brand 1977, 54).

Not surprisingly, a few days after landing, the first space
shuttle astronauts were greeted by Elder Neal Maxwell at the
Mormon Tabernacle. "We honor tonight men who have seen

God in all his majesty and power," he said, and the six-thousand-member congregation responded, "Amen."

Viewed from this perspective, the fight between creationism and evolutionism appears as an internal capitalist debate to determine the most adequate means of control. Until our social biologists and genetic engineers—the heroes of today's scientific breakthrough—have discovered the means to create a perfect robot, the whip will do, particularly in an age still infected with the anarchic/subversive ideologies of the 1960s.

Moreover, asceticism, self-control, the flight from the earth and the body—the substance of puritan teaching—are the best soil in which capital's scientific and economic plans can flourish. Quite consciously, in its attempt to relocate itself on safer shores, capital is embracing the dream of all religion: the overcoming of all physical boundaries, the reduction of human beings to angel-like creatures, all soul and will.[1] In the creation of the electronic/space worker, the priest of scientific exploration-exploitation of the universe, capital is fighting once again its historic battle against matter, attempting to break at once both the boundaries of the earth and the boundaries of "human nature" which, in its current form, present irreducible limits that must be overcome.

The planned organization of industries in space and the dematerialization of the body go together. For the former cannot be accomplished without the remolding of a whole nexus of needs, wishes, and desires, which are the product of billions of years of material evolution on the planet and up to now have been the material conditions of our biosocial reproduction: the blues, the greens, the nipple, the balls, the texture of oranges, beef, carrots, the winds and the sea smell, the daylight, the need for physical contact, SEX! The dangers of sexual desire are emblematic of the obstacles capital encounters in the attempt to create totally self-controlled beings, capable of spending nights and nights alone, just talking to their computers, their mind focused on nothing but the screen. Can you afford to be horny or lonely in space? Can you afford to be jealous or have a marital breakdown?

The right attitude in this respect is indicated by a report on the South Pole Station in Antarctica that was ostensibly set up to study meteorological, astronomical, and geographical conditions at the pole but actually functioned as a center for human experimentation: the study of human beings in conditions approaching that of space (isolation for many months, lack of sensuous contact, etc.). According to the report: "All candidates were warned of the 'dangers' of sexual liaisons under the supercharged conditions here. Celibacy was the best course.... Men think of nothing but sex for the first few weeks, then it is submerged until nearly the end of the winter. [One worker reported,] 'You just basically put it out of your mind. You are working all the time; there is no privacy'" (Reinhold 1982).[2]

Celibacy, abstinence: this is the last step in a long process whereby capital has decreased the sensuous-sexual content of our lives and encounters with people, substituting the mental image for the physical touch. Centuries of capitalist discipline have gone a long way toward producing individuals who shrink from each other for fear of touch. (See the way we live our social spaces: buses, trains, each passenger closed in their own space, keeping well-defined though invisible boundaries; each person their own castle. Doctors too seldom touch our bodies any longer, only relying for their diagnoses on lab reports). This physical as well as emotional isolation from each other, which communication through computers and cell phones intensify, is the essence and new form of capitalist cooperation. But this trend toward the dematerialization of all forms of our life culminates in the imagined inhabitants of future space colonies whose success depends on their ability to become angels, who do not require the sensuous stimulations that are our daily nourishment on earth but can live solely by feeding on their self-sufficient, self-centered willpower.

The abstractness of life is matched by the abstractness of death. In today's wars the enemy's body is a blip on a screen whose destruction is as simple as playing a video game. Here too a religious training, dividing humanity into elected and damned, is crucial. It is a small step from accepting the necessity of hellfire to accepting the destruction of other bodies—even millions in a nuclear war—as a means to cleanse the earth from all social deviation. Breaking all bonds between ourselves and others and distancing ourselves even from our own body is a first step. We thus have the electronic church that dematerializes the healer—appearing as an image on thousands of screens and an address to which to send the money so that he presumably prays for you.

Indeed, sounds and images are replacing social relations. They substitute unpredictable human encounters with a techno-sociality that can be activated and terminated at will. Living with the machine and becoming like a machine is of the essence. The ideal type is a desexualized angel, moving in the interstices of the engine, perfectly integrating work-space and life space as in the astronauts' pod, weightless because purified of the force of gravity exercised by human desires and temptations—the refusal of work finally negated. Capital's old dream of human perfectibility, that loomed so prominent in the sixteenth- and seventeenth-century utopias, from Bacon to Descartes, seems ready at hand. Here is Wally Schirra, the NASA astronaut who in 1968 piloted the Apollo 7, speaking of his experience in space:

> Feeling weightless . . . I don't know, it's so many things together. A feeling of pride, of healthy solitude, of dignified freedom from everything that's dirty, sticky. You feel exquisitely comfortable, that's the word for it, exquisitely. . . . You feel comfortable and you feel you have so much energy, such an urge to do things, such an ability to do things. And you work well, yes, you think

well, you move well, without sweat, without difficulty, as if the biblical curse "In the sweat of thy face and in sorrow" no longer exists. As if you've been born again.[3]

No wonder capital is so careless with our earthly home and so ready to destroy it in nuclear explosions—perfect embodiment of the victory of the spirit over the earth-matter—as creative as the first act of God! Big Bang, Big Phallus reduced to its power-hungry essence, dismembering this earth of mankind in its god-like aspiration to be free from all constraints. Faust in an astronaut/space-worker suit, a superman who does not need any-body, determined to have his will, not just on earth but in the universe as well.

A society of angels motivated by religious-patriotic concerns. The adventure of space colonization will not be a "New America," however, in the sense of being a ground populated by castaways, indentured servants, and slaves. The need for total identification with the work-project, total obedience, total self-discipline and self-control, is so high that, according to NASA, even the old forms of reward should be ruled out: "High monetary incentive should not be used for space colonization recruiting, because it attracts the wrong people" (Johnson and Holbrow 1977, 31). Work without a wage. This is the ultimate capitalist utopia, work becoming its own reward and all refusers are cast out into the cold stellar night. Capitalism has finally reached its goal and its limit.

Notes

1 See on this subject Sol Yurick, *Behold Metatron, the Recording Angel* (1985).
2 Robert Reinhold, "Strife and Despair at South Pole Illuminate Psychology of Isolation," *New York Times*, January 12, 1982.
3 A quote from Walter M. Schirra Jr. during a television broadcast from space in the Apollo 7 in October 1968.

PART FOUR

TEN

In Praise of the Dancing Body

The history of the body is the history of human beings, for there is no cultural practice that is not first applied to the body. Even if we limit ourselves to speak of the history of the body in capitalism, we face an overwhelming task, so extensive have been the techniques used to discipline the body, constantly changing, depending on the shifts in the different labor regimes to which our body was subjected.

A history of the body can be reconstructed by describing the different forms of repression that capitalism has activated against it. But I have decided to write instead of the body as a ground of resistance, that is, the body and its powers—the power to act, to transform itself and the body as a limit on exploitation.

There is something we have lost in our insistence on the body as something socially constructed and performative. The view of the body as a social (discursive) production has hidden the fact that our body is a receptacle of powers, capacities, and resistances that have been developed in a long process of coevolution with our natural environment as well as intergenerational practices that have made it a natural limit to exploitation.

By the body as a "natural limit" I refer to the structure of needs and desires created in us not only by our conscious decisions or collective practices but also by millions of years of material evolution: the need for the sun, for the blue sky and the green of trees, for the smell of the woods and the oceans, the need for touching, smelling, sleeping, making love.

This accumulated structure of needs and desires, that for thousands of years has been the condition of our social reproduction, has put limits on our exploitation and is something that capitalism has incessantly struggled to overcome.

Capitalism was not the first system based on the exploitation of human labor. But more than any other system in history, it has tried to create an economic world where labor is the most essential principle of accumulation. As such it was the first to make the regimentation and mechanization of the body a key premise of the accumulation of wealth. Indeed, one of capitalism's main social tasks from its beginning to the present has been the transformation of our energies and corporeal powers into labor powers.

In *Caliban and the Witch* (2004), I have looked at the strategies that capitalism has employed to accomplish this task and remold human nature, in the same way as it has tried to remold the earth in order to make the land more productive and to turn animals into living factories. I have spoken of the historic battle it has waged against the body, against our materiality, and the many institutions it has created for this purpose: the law, the whip, the regulation of sexuality, as well as myriad social practices that have redefined our relation to space, to nature, and to each other.

Capitalism was born from the separation of people from the land, and its first task was to make work independent of the seasons and to lengthen the workday beyond the limits of our endurance. Generally, we stress the economic aspect of this process, the economic dependence that capitalism has created on monetary relations, and its role in the formation of a wage proletariat. What we have not always seen is what the separation from the land and nature has meant for our body, which has been pauperized and stripped of the powers that precapitalist populations attributed to it.

Nature, as Marx (1988, 75–76) recognized it, is our "inorganic body," and there was a time when we could read the winds, the clouds, and the changes in the currents of rivers and seas. In precapitalist societies people thought they had the power to fly, to have out-of-body experiences, to communicate, to speak with animals, take on their powers, and even shape-shift. They also thought that they could be in more places than one and, for example, come back from the grave to take revenge of their enemies.

Not all these powers were imaginary. Daily contact with nature was the source of a great amount of knowledge reflected in the food revolution that took place especially in the Americas prior to colonization or in the revolution in sailing techniques. We know now, for instance, that the Polynesian populations used to travel the high seas at night with only their bodies as their compass, as they could tell from the vibrations of the waves the different ways by which they could direct their boats to the shore.

Fixation in space and time has been one of the most elementary and persistent techniques capitalism has used to take hold of the body. See the attacks throughout history on vagabonds, migrants, and hobos. Mobility is a threat when not pursued for the sake of work, as it circulates knowledge, experiences, struggles. In the past the instruments of restraint were whips, chains, the stocks, mutilation, enslavement. Today, in addition to the whip and the detention centers, we have computer surveillance and the periodic threat of epidemics such as avian flu as a means of controlling nomadism.

Mechanization—the turning of the body, male and female, into a machine—has been one of capitalism's most relentless pursuits. Animals too are turned into machines, so that sows can double their litter, chicken can produce uninterrupted flows of eggs, while unproductive ones are ground up, and calves can never stand on their feet before being brought to the slaughterhouse. I cannot here evoke all the ways in which the mechanization of body has occurred. Enough to say that the techniques of capture and domination have changed depending on the dominant labor regime and the machines that have been the model for the body.

Thus, we find that in the sixteenth and seventeenth centuries (the time of manufacture) the body was imagined and disciplined according to the model of simple machines, like the pump and the lever. This was the regime that culminated in Taylorism, time-motion study, where every motion was calculated and all energies were channeled to the task.

Resistance here was imagined in the form of inertia, with the body pictured as a dumb animal, a monster resistant to command.

With the nineteenth century we have, instead, a conception of the body and disciplinary techniques modeled on the steam engine, its productivity calculated in terms of input and output, and *efficiency* becoming the key word. Under this regime, the disciplining of the body was accomplished through dietary restrictions and the calculation of the calories that a working body would need. The climax, in this context, was the Nazi table that specified what calories each type of worker needed. The enemy here was the dispersion of energy, entropy, waste, disorder. In the US, the history of this new political economy began in the 1880s, with the attack on the saloon and the remolding of family life with at its center the full-time housewife, conceived as an anti-entropic device, always on call, ready to restore the meal consumed, the bodies sullied after the bath, the dress repaired and torn again.

In our time, models for the body are the computer and the genetic code, crafting a dematerialized, disaggregated body, imagined as a conglomerate of cells and genes, each with their own program, unconcerned with the rest and the good of the body as a whole. Such is the theory of the "selfish gene"—the idea that the body is made of individualistic cells and genes all pursuing their program, a perfect metaphor of the neoliberal conception of life, where market dominance turns against not only group solidarity but solidarity within ourselves. Consistently, the body disintegrates into an assemblage of selfish genes, each striving to achieve its selfish goals, indifferent to the interest of the rest.

To the extent that we internalize this view, we internalize the most profound experience of self-alienation, as we confront not only a great beast that does not obey our orders but also a host of micro-enemies that are planted right into our own body, ready to attack us at any moment. Industries have been built on the fears that this conception of the body generates, putting us at the mercy of forces that we do not control. Inevitably, if we internalize this view, we do not taste good to ourselves. In fact, our body scares us, and we do not listen to it. We do not hear what it wants but join the assault on it with all the weapons that medicine can offer: radiation, colonoscopy, mammography, all arms in a long battle against the body, with us joining in the assault rather than taking our body out of the line of fire. In this way, we are prepared to accept a world that transforms body parts into commodities for a market and view our body as a repository of diseases: the body as plague, the body as source of epidemics, the body without reason.

Our struggle then must begin with the reappropriation of our body, the revaluation and rediscovery of its capacity for resistance, and expansion and celebration of its powers, individual and collective.

Dance is central to this reappropriation. In essence, the act of dancing is an exploration and invention of what a body can do: of its capacities, its languages, its articulations of the strivings of our being. I have come to believe that there is a philosophy in dancing, for dance mimics the processes by which we relate to the world, connect with other bodies, transform ourselves and the space around us. From dance we learn that matter is not stupid, it is not blind, it is not mechanical but has its rhythms, its language, and it is self-activated and self-organizing. Our bodies have reasons that we need to learn, rediscover, reinvent. We need to listen to their language as the path to our health and healing, as we need to listen to the language and rhythms of the natural world as the path to the health and healing of the earth. Since the power to be affected and to effect, to be moved and to move, a capacity that is indestructible, exhausted only with death, is constitutive of the body, there is an immanent politics residing in it: the capacity to transform itself, others, and change the world.

AFTERWORD

On Joyful Militancy

The principle of joyful militancy is that either our politics are liberating, either they change our life in a way that is positive, that make us grow, give us joy, or there's something wrong with them.

Sad politics often come from an exaggerated sense of what we can do by ourselves, individually, which leads to the habit of overburdening ourselves. I am reminded here of Nietzsche's metamorphoses in *Thus Spoke Zarathustra*, where he describes the camel as the beast of burden, the embodiment of the spirit of gravity. The camel is the prototype of the militants who are always loaded with huge amounts of work, because they think that the destiny of the world depends upon them. The heroic, Stakhanovite militants are always sad because they try to do so much that they are never fully present to what they are doing, never fully present to their lives and cannot appreciate the transformative possibilities of their political work. When we work this way, we are also frustrated because we are not transformed by what we do, and we have no time to change our relations with the people we are working with.

The mistake is setting goals that we cannot reach and always fighting "against" rather than trying to construct something. This means that we are always projected toward the future, whereas a joyful politics is constructive already in the present. More people today see that. We cannot place our goals into a future that is constantly receding. We need to set goals that we can achieve in part also in the present, though our horizon must be obviously broader. Being politically active must positively change our life and our relations with people around us. Sadness comes when we continually postpone what is to be achieved to a future that we never see coming, and as a result we are blind to what is possible in the present.

I also object to the notion of self-sacrifice. I don't believe in sacrifice, if it means that we have to repress ourselves, that we do things that go against our needs, our desires, our potential. This is not to say that political work will not lead to suffering. But there is a difference between suffering because something we have decided to do has painful consequences—like facing repression, seeing people we care for hurt—and self-sacrifice, which is doing something against our desire and will, only because we think that it is our duty. This makes for unhappy, dissatisfied individuals. Doing political work must be healing. It must give us strength, vision, enhance our sense of solidarity, and make us realize our interdependence. Being able to politicize our pain, turn it into a source of knowledge, into something that connects us to other people—all of this has a healing power. It is "empowering" (a word, however, I have come to dislike).

I believe that the radical Left has often failed to attract people because it does not pay attention to the reproductive side of political work—the dinners together, the songs that strengthen our sense of being a collective subject, the affective relations we develop among each other. The indigenous people of the Americas teach us, for instance, how important the fiestas are as means not simply of recreation but also of solidarity building, of resignification of our mutual affection and responsibility. They teach us the importance of activities that bring people together, that make us feel the warmth of solidarity and build trust. Thus, they take the organization of fiestas very seriously. For all their limits, workers' organizations in the past fulfilled this function, building centers where (male) workers would go after work, to drink a glass of wine, meet with comrades, pick up the latest news and plans for action. In this way politics created an extended family, the transmission of knowledge among the different generations was guaranteed, and politics itself acquired a different meaning. This has not been the culture of the Left, not at least in our time, and that is partly where sadness often comes in. Political work should change our relations with people, strengthen our connectedness, give us courage in the knowledge that we are not confronting the world alone.

I prefer to speak of joy rather than happiness. I prefer joy because it is an active passion. It is not a stagnant state of being. It is not satisfaction with things as they are. It is feeling our powers, seeing our capacities growing in ourselves and in the people around us. This is a feeling that comes from a process of transformation. It means, using Spinoza's language, that we understand the situation we are in and are moving along in accordance to what is required of us in that moment. So we feel that we have the power to change and that we are changing, together with other people. It's not acquiescence to what exists.

Spinoza speaks of joy as coming from reason and understanding. An important step here is understanding that we come to the movement with many scars. We all bear the marks of life in a capitalist society. This, in fact, is why we want to struggle, change the world. There would be no need for it if we could be perfect human beings—whatever this may mean—already in this society. But we are often disappointed because we imagine that in the movement we must find only harmonious relations, and instead we often encounter jealousies, backbiting, unequal power relations.

In the women's movement too we can experience painful and disappointing relations. In fact, it is in women's groups and organizations that we are most likely to experience deepest disappointments and pains. For we may expect to be let down and betrayed by men, but we do not expect that from women, and we do not imagine that as women we can also hurt each other, we can feel devalued, unseen, or make other women feel this way. There are obviously times when behind the personal conflicts there are unacknowledged political differences that it may not be possible to overcome. But it is also possible that we feel betrayed and become heartbroken because we assume that being in a radical movement and above all being in a feminist movement is a guarantee of liberation from all the wounds that we carry in our bodies and souls, and therefore we let our defense down in a way we would never do in our personal relations with men or in mixed organizations. Inevitably sadness sets in, at times to the point that we decide to leave. With time we learn that the pettiness, the jealousies, the excessive vulnerabilities we often meet in women's movements are often part of the distortion that life in a capitalist society creates. It is part of our political growth to learn to identify them and not be destroyed by them.

References

Acton, William. (1857) 1969. *Prostitution*. New York: Praeger.

Apfel, Alana. 2016. *Birth Work as Care Work: Stories from Activist Birth Communities*. Oakland: PM Press.

Arditti, Rita, Renate Klein, and Shelley Minden, eds. 1984. *Test-Tube Women: What Future for Motherhood?* London: Pandora Press.

Baggesen, Lise Haller. 2014. *Mothernism*. Chicago: Green Lantern Press.

Barnes, Barry, and Steven Shapin, eds., 1979. *Natural Order: Historical Studies of Scientific Culture*. Beverly Hills, CA: Sage.

Beauvoir, Simone de. 1989. *The Second Sex*. New York: Vintage Books. Translated from the French *Le Deuxième Sexe*. Gallimard, 1949.

Beckles, Hilary McD. 1989. *Natural Rebels: A Social History of Enslaved Black Women in Barbados*. New Brunswick, NJ: Rutgers University Press.

Berardi, Franco. 2009a. *Precarious Rhapsody: Semiocapitalism and Pathologies of the Post-Alpha Generation*. London: Minor Composition.

———. 2009b. *The Soul at Work: From Alienation to Autonomy*. Los Angeles: Semiotext(e).

Bernasconi, Robert. 2001. "Who Invented the Concept of Race?" In *Race*, edited by Robert Bernasconi, 11–36. Malden, MA: Blackwell.

Bordo, Susan. 1993. *Unbearable Weight: Feminism, Western Culture and the Body*. Berkeley: University of California Press.

Boston Women's Health Book Collective. 1976. *Our Bodies, Ourselves: A Book by and for Women*. New York: Simon and Schuster. First published 1971.

Bowring, Finn. 2003. *Science, Seeds, and Cyborgs: Biotechnology and the Appropriation of Life*. London: Verso.

Brand, Stewart, ed. 1977. *Space Colonies*. New York: Penguin.

Braverman, Harry. 1974. *Labor and Monopoly Capital: The Degradation of Work in the Twentieth Century*. New York: Monthly Review.

Briggs, Laura. 2002. *Reproducing Empire: Race, Sex, Science, and U.S. Imperialism in Puerto Rico*. Berkeley: University of California Press.

Brown, J.A.C. 1954. *The Social Psychology of Industry*. London: Pelican.

Brown, Jenny. 2018. *Birth Strike: The Hidden Fight over Women's Work*. Oakland: PM Press.

Butchart, Alexander. 1998. *The Anatomy of Power: European Constructions of the African Body*. London: Zed Books.

Butler, Judith. 1993. *Bodies That Matter: On the Discursive Limits of Sex*. New York: Routledge.

———. 1999. *Gender Trouble: Feminism and the Subversion of Identity*. New York: Routledge.

———. 2004. *Undoing Gender*. New York: Routledge.

Caffentzis, George. 2000. *Exciting the Industry of Mankind: George's Berkeley's Philosophy of Money*. Dortrecht: Kluwer.

———. 2012. *In Letters of Blood and Fire: Work, Machines, and the Crisis of Capitalism*. Oakland: PM Press.

———. Forthcoming. *Civilizing Money: David Hume's Philosophy of Money*.

Carlsson, Chris. 2008. *Nowtopia: How Pirate Programmers, Outlaw Bicyclists, and Vacant-Lot Gardeners Are Inventing the Future Today*. Oakland: AK Press.

Connelly, Matthew. 2008. *Fatal Mis-Conception: The Struggle to Control World Population*. Cambridge, MA: The Belknap Press of Harvard University Press.

Corea, Gena. 1979. *The Mother Machine: Reproductive Technologies from Artificial Insemination to Artificial Wombs*. New York: Harper and Row.

Cott, Nancy. 1972. *Root of Bitterness: Documents of the Social History of American Women*. New York: E.P. Dutton.

Danna, Daniela. 2015. *Contract Children: Questioning Surrogacy*. Stuttgart: Ibidem-Verlag.

———. 2019. *Il peso dei numeri: Teorie e dinamiche della popolazione*. Trieste: Asterios Editore.

Danner, Mona J. E. , 2012, "Three Strikes and It's Women Who Are Out: The Hidden Consequences for Women of Criminal Justice Policy Reforms." In *It's a Crime: Women and Justice*, edited by Roslyn Muraskin, 354–64. 5th ed. Boston: Prentice Hall.

Davis, Angela. 1998. "Surrogates and Outcast Mothers: Racism and Reproductive Policies in the Nineties." In *The Angela Y. Davis Reader*, edited by Joy James, 210–21. Malden, MA: Blackwell.

Deleuze, Gilles. 1997. *Negotiations: 1972–1990*. New York: Columbia University Press.

Diepenbrock, Chloé. 2000. "God Willed It! Gynecology at the Checkout Stand: Reproductive Technology in the Women's Service Magazine, 1977–1996." In *Body Talk: Rhetoric, Technology, Reproduction*, edited by Mary M. Lay et al., 98–121. Madison: University of Wisconsin Press.

Ehrenreich, Barbara. 2001. "Welcome to Cancerland: A Mammogram Leads to a Cult of Pink Kitsch." *Harper's Magazine*, November 2001, 43–53.

———. 2018. *Natural Causes: An Epidemic of Wellness, the Certainty of Dying, and Killing Ourselves to Live Longer*. New York: Hachette Book Group.

Ehrenreich, Barbara, and Deirdre English. 2010. *Witches, Midwives and Nurses: A History of Women Healers*. 2nd ed. New York: The Feminist Press at CUNY. First published 1973.

Fanon, Frantz. 1967. *Black Skin, White Masks*. New York: Grove Press.

Fausto-Sterling, Anne. 2000. *Sexing the Body: Gender Politics and the Construction of Sexuality*. Boston: Basic Books.

Federici, Silvia. 2004. *Caliban and the Witch: Women, the Body and Primitive Accumulation*. Brooklyn: Autonomedia.

———. 2012. *Revolution at Point Zero: Reproduction, Housework and Feminist Struggle*. Oakland: PM Press.

———. 2018. *Witches, Witch-Hunting, and Women*. Oakland: PM Press.

Firestone, Shulamith. 1970. *The Dialectic of Sex: The Case for Feminist Revolution*. London: Woman's Press.

Foucault, Michel. 1978. *A History of Sexuality*. Vol. 1, *An Introduction*. New York: Penguin. Translated from the French *La Volonté de Savoir*. Gallimard, 1976.

———. 1979. *Discipline and Punish: The Birth of the Prison*. New York: Vintage Books. Translated from the French *Surveiller et Punir: Naissance de la Prison*. Gallimard, 1975.

Fox, Meg. 1989. "Unreliable Allies: Subjective and Objective Time in Childbirth." In *Taking Our Time: Feminist Perspectives on Temporality*, edited by Frieda Johles Forman with Caoran Sowton, 123–35. Oxford: Pergamon Press.

Freud, Sigmund. 1973. *Sexuality and the Psychology of Love*. New York: Collier.

Gargallo Celentani, Francesca. 2013. *Feminismo desde Abya Yala: Ideas y proposiciones de las mujeres de 607 pueblos en nuestra América*. Buenos Aires: América Libre–Chichimora Editorial.

Ginsburg, Faye D., and Rayna Rapp, eds. 1995. *Conceiving the New World Order: The Global Politics of Reproduction*. Berkeley: University of California Press.

Greenberg, Gary. 2010. "The War on Unhappiness." *Harper's Magazine*, September 2010: 27–35.

Guattari, Félix. 1996. *Soft Subversions*. Edited by Silvère Lotringer. New York: Semiotext(e).

Haley, Sarah. 2016. *No Mercy Here: Gender, Punishment, and the Making of Jim Crow Modernity*. Chapel Hill: University of North Carolina Press.

Haller Baggesen, Lise. 2014. *Mothernism*. Chicago: Green Lantern Press.

Hanmer, Jalna. 1983. "Reproductive Technology: The Future for Women?" In *Machina ex Dea: Feminist Perspectives on Technology*, edited by Joan Rothschild, 183–97. New York: Pergamon Press.

Haraway, Donna J. 1991. "Cyborg Manifesto." In *Simians, Cyborgs, and Women: The Reinvention of Nature*. New York: Routledge.

Harcourt, Wendy. 2009. *Body Politics in Development*. London: Zed Books.

Harris, Wess, ed. 2017. *Written in Blood: Courage and Corruption in the Appalachian War of Extraction*. Oakland: PM Press.

Hartmann, Betsy. 1995. *Reproductive Rights and Wrongs: The Global Politics of Population Control*. Boston: South End Press.

Hobbes, Thomas. 1651. *Leviathan*. London: Crooke.

hooks, bell. 1981. *Ain't I a Woman: Black Women and Feminism*. Boston: South End Press.

———. 1988. *Talking Back: Thinking Feminism, Thinking Black*. Toronto: Boston: South End Press.

———. 1990. *Yearning: Race, Gender, and Cultural Politics*. Boston: South End Press,

Hornblum, Allen M., Judith L. Newman, and Gregory J. Dober. 2013. *Against Their Will: The Secret History of Medical Experimentation on Children in Cold War America*. New York: St. Martin's Press.

Johles Forman, Frieda, ed., with Caoran Sowton. 1989. *Taking Our Time: Feminist Perspectives on Temporality*. New York: Pergamon Press.

Johnson, Richard, and Charles H. Holbrow, eds. 1977. *Space Settlements: A Design Study*. Washington, DC: NASA, Scientific and Technical Information Office.

Jones, James H. 1993. *Bad Blood: The Tuskegee Syphilis Experiment.* New York: Free Press. First published 1981.

Jones, Jesse. 2017. *Tremble, Tremble / Tremate, Tremate.* Dublin: Project Press; Milan: Mousse Publishing.

Komarovsky, Mirra. 1967. *Blue-Collar Marriage.* New York: Vintage Books.

Laqueur, Thomas. 1990. *Making Sex: Body and Gender from the Greeks to Freud.* Cambridge, MA: Harvard University Press.

Lay, Mary M. et al., eds. 2000. *Body Talk: Rhetoric, Technology, Reproduction.* Madison: University of Wisconsin Press.

LeFlouria, Talitha L. 2016. *Chained in Silence: Black Women and Convict Labor in the New South.* Chapel Hill: University of North Carolina Press.

Le Sueur, Meridel. 1984. *Women on the Breadlines.* Minneapolis: West End Press. First published 1977.

Levidow, Les, and Kevin Robins. 1989. *Cyborg World: The Military Information Society.* London: Free Association Books.

Linebaugh, Peter. 1992. *The London Hanged: Crime and Civil Society in the 18th Century.* Cambridge: Cambridge University Press.

Locke, John. (1689) 1959. *An Essay Concerning Human Understanding.* Vol. 1. New York: Dover.

Lombroso, Cesare, and Guglielmo Ferrero. (1893) 2004. *Criminal Woman, the Prostitute, and the Normal Woman.* Durham, NC: Duke University Press.

Lyubomirsky, Sonja, Laura King, and Ed Diener. 2005. "The Benefits of Frequent Positive Effect: Does Happiness Lead to Success?" *Psychological Bulletin* 131, no. 6, 803–55.

Mac, Juno, and Molly Smith. 2018. *Revolting Prostitutes: The Fight for Sex Workers' Rights.* London: Verso.

Marshall, Alfred. (1890) 1990. *Principles of Economics.* Philadelphia: Porcupine Press.

Marx, Karl. 1988. *Economic and Philosophical Manuscripts of 1844.* Translated by Martin Milligan. Buffalo: Prometheus Books.

———. 1990. *Capital.* Vol. 1. London: Penguin.

Melossi, Dario, and Massimo Pavarini. 1981. *The Prison and the Factory: Origin of the Penitentiary System.* Totowa, NJ: Barnes and Noble.

Merino, Patricia. 2017. *Maternidad, Igualdad y Fraternidad: Las madres como sujeto político en las sociedades poslaborales.* Madrid: Clave Intelectual.

Mies, Maria. 2014. *Patriarchy and Accumulation on a World Scale: Women in the International Division of Labor.* London: Zed Books. First published 1986.

Milwaukee County Welfare Rights Organization. 1972. *Welfare Mothers Speak Out: We Ain't Gonna Shuffle Anymore*. New York: Norton.

Molina, Natalia. 2006. *Fit to Be Citizens: Public Health and Race, 1879–1939*. Berkeley: University of California Press.

Moraga, Cherríe, and Gloria Anzaldúa, eds. 1983. *This Bridge Called My Back*. New York: Kitchen Table: Women of Color Press.

Morgan, Robin. 1970. *Sisterhood Is Powerful: An Anthology of Writings from the Women's Liberation Movement*. New York, Random House.

Murphy, Julien S. 1995. *The Constructed Body: AIDS, Reproductive Technology, and Ethics*. New York: SUNY Press.

Nissim, Rina. 2014. *Une sorcière des temps modernes: Le self-help et le mouvement femmes et santé*. Lausanne: Editions Mamamélis.

Noble, David F. 1999. *The Religion of Technology: The Divinity of Man and the Spirit of Invention*. New York: Penguin.

Nourse, Victoria F. 2008. *In Reckless Hands. Skinner v. Oklahoma and the Near Triumph of American Eugenics*. New York: W.W. Norton.

O'Neill, William L. 1967. *Divorce in the Progressive Era*. New Haven, CT: Yale University Press.

Paltrow Lynn M., and Jeanne Flavin. 2013. "Arrests and Forced Interventions on Pregnant Women in the United States, 1973–2005: Implications for Women's Legal Status and Public Health." *Journal of Health Politics, Policy and Law* 38, no. 2 (April): 299–343.

Pateman, Carole. 1988. *The Sexual Contract*. Stanford, CA: Stanford University Press.

Pfeufer Kahn, Robbie. 1989. "Women and Time in Childbirth and Lactation." In *Taking Our Time: Feminist Perspectives on Temporality*, edited by Frieda Johles Forman with Caoran Sowton, 20–36. New York: Pergamon Press.

Polhemus, Ted. 1978. *The Body Reader: Social Aspects of the Human Body*. New York: Pantheon.

Poole, W. Scott. 2009. *Satan in America: The Devil We Know*. Rowman and Littlefield.

Reese, Ellen. 2005. *Backlash against Welfare Mothers: Past and Present*. Berkeley: University of California Press.

Reinhold, Robert. 1982. "Strife and Despair at South Pole Illuminate Psychology of Isolation." *New York Times*, January 12, 1982.

Roberts, Dorothy. (1997) 2017. *Killing the Black Body: Race, Reproduction, and the Meaning of Liberty*. New York: Vintage Books.

Rothschild, Joan ed. 1983. *Machina Ex Dea: Feminist Perspectives on Technology*. New York: Pergamon Press.

Rozzi, R.A. 1975. *Psicologi e Operai: Soggettività e lavoro nell'industria italiana*. Milan: Feltrinelli.

Rynes, Sara L., Barry Gerhart, and Laura Parks-Leduc. 2005. "Personnel Psychology: Performance Evaluation and Pay for Performance." *Annual Review of Psychology* 56, no. 1 (February): 571–600.

Salecl, Renata. 2004. *On Anxiety*. New York: Routledge.

Sartre, Jean-Paul. 1956. *Being and Nothingness: A Phenomenological Essay on Ontology*. New York: Pocket Books. Translated from the French *L'être et le néant*. Gallimard, 1953.

———. 1976. *No Exit and Three Other Plays*. New York: Vintage Books. Translated from the French *Huis Clos*. Gallimard, 1945.

Schiebinger, Londa. 2004. *Nature's Body: Gender in the Making of Modern Science*. New Brunswick, NJ: Rutgers University Press. First published 1993.

Seidman, Steven. 1997. *Difference Troubles. Queering Social Theory and Sexual Politics*. Cambridge: Cambridge University Press.

Solinger, Rickie, et al., eds., 2010. *Interrupted Lives: Experiences of Incarcerated Women in the United States*. Berkeley: University of California Press

Starr, Paul. 1982. *The Social Transformation of American Medicine*. New York: Basic Books.

Stocking, George W., Jr. 1988. *Bones, Bodies, Behavior: Essays on Biological Anthropology*. Madison: University of Wisconsin Press.

Sublette, Ned, and Constance Sublette. 2016. *The American Slave Coast: A History of the Breeding Industry*. Chicago: Lawrence Hill.

Tajima-Pena, Renee, director and producer. 2015. *No Más Bebés / No More Babies*. San Francisco: ITVS; Los Angeles: Moon Canyon Films.

Tapia, Ruby C. 2010. "Representing the Experience of Incarcerated Women in the United States." In *Interrupted Lives: Experiences of Incarcerated Women in the United States*, edited by Rickie Solinger, 1–6. Berkeley: University of California Press.

Taylor, Sunaura. 2017. *Beasts of Burden: Animal and Disability Liberation*. New York: New Press.

Townley, Chiara. 2019. "Cosmetic Surgery Is on the Rise, New Data Reveal." *Medical News*, March 17, 2019.

Turner, Bryan S. 1992. *Regulating Bodies: Essays in Medical Sociology*. London: Routledge.

Turney, Lyn. 2000. "The Politics of Language in Surgical Contraception." In *Body Talk: Rhetoric, Technology, Reproduction*, edited by Mary M. Lay et al., 161–83. Madison: University of Wisconsin Press.

Twohey, Megan. 2013. "Americans Use the Internet to Abandon Children Adopted from Overseas." Reuters investigative report, The Child Exchange: Inside America's Underground Market for Adopted Children, part 1 (September 9). https://www.reuters.com/investigates/adoption/#article/part1.

Valentine, David. 2007. *Imagining Transgender: An Ethnography of a Category*. Durham, NC: Duke University Press.

Welsome, Eileen. 1993. "*The Plutonium Experiment.*" *Albuquerque Tribune*, November 15–17, 1993.

Williams, Kristian. 2006. *American Methods: Torture and the Logic of Domination*. Boston: South End Press.

Wittig, Monique. 1992. "The Straight Mind." In *The Straight Mind and Other Essays*, 21–32. New York: Harvester Wheatsheaf.

Yurick, Sol. 1985. *Behold Metatron, the Recording Angel*. Brooklyn: Autonomedia.

About the Author

Silvia Federici is a feminist writer, teacher, and militant. In 1972, she was cofounder of the International Feminist Collective, which launched the Wages for Housework campaign.

In the 1990s, after a period of teaching and research in Nigeria, she was active in the anti-globalization movement and the U.S. anti–death penalty movement. She is one of the cofounders of the Committee for Academic Freedom in Africa. From 1987 to 2005, she taught international studies, women's studies, and political philosophy courses at Hofstra University in Hempstead, NY.

Her research and political organizing accompany a long list of publications on philosophy and feminist theory, women's history, education, culture, international politics, and the worldwide struggle against capitalist globalization and for a feminist reconstruction of the commons. Federici's steadfast commitment to these issues resounds in her focus on autonomy and her emphasis on the power of what she calls self-reproducing movements as a challenge to capitalism through the construction of new social relations. Her most recent books are *Witches, Witch-Hunting, and Women*; *Re-enchanting the World*; and *The Patriarchy of the Wage*.

ABOUT PM PRESS

PM Press is an independent, radical publisher of books and media to educate, entertain, and inspire. Founded in 2007 by a small group of people with decades of publishing, media, and organizing experience, PM Press amplifies the voices of radical authors, artists, and activists. Our aim is to deliver bold political ideas and vital stories to all walks of life and arm the dreamers to demand the impossible. We have sold millions of copies of our books, most often one at a time, face to face. We're old enough to know what we're doing and young enough to know what's at stake. Join us to create a better world.

PM Press
PO Box 23912
Oakland, CA 94623
www.pmpress.org

PM Press in Europe
europe@pmpress.org
www.pmpress.org.uk

FRIENDS OF PM PRESS

These are indisputably momentous times—the financial system is melting down globally and the Empire is stumbling. Now more than ever there is a vital need for radical ideas.

In the years since its founding—and on a mere shoestring—PM Press has risen to the formidable challenge of publishing and distributing knowledge and entertainment for the struggles ahead. With over 450 releases to date, we have published an impressive and stimulating array of literature, art, music, politics, and culture. Using every available medium, we've succeeded in connecting those hungry for ideas and information to those putting them into practice.

Friends of PM allows you to directly help impact, amplify, and revitalize the discourse and actions of radical writers, filmmakers, and artists. It provides us with a stable foundation from which we can build upon our early successes and provides a much-needed subsidy for the materials that can't necessarily pay their own way. You can help make that happen—and receive every new title automatically delivered to your door once a month—by joining as a Friend of PM Press. And, we'll throw in a free T-shirt when you sign up.

Here are your options:

- **$30 a month** Get all books and pamphlets plus 50% discount on all webstore purchases

- **$40 a month** Get all PM Press releases (including CDs and DVDs) plus 50% discount on all webstore purchases

- **$100 a month** Superstar—Everything plus PM merchandise, free downloads, and 50% discount on all webstore purchases

For those who can't afford $30 or more a month, we have **Sustainer Rates** at $15, $10 and $5. Sustainers get a free PM Press T-shirt and a 50% discount on all purchases from our website.

Your Visa or Mastercard will be billed once a month, until you tell us to stop. Or until our efforts succeed in bringing the revolution around. Or the financial meltdown of Capital makes plastic redundant. Whichever comes first.

DEPARTMENT OF ANTHROPOLOGY & SOCIAL CHANGE

Anthropology and Social Change, housed within the California Institute of Integral Studies, is a small innovative graduate department with a particular focus on activist scholarship, militant research, and social change. We offer both masters and doctoral degree programs.

Our unique approach to collaborative research methodology dissolves traditional barriers between research and political activism, between insiders and outsiders, and between researchers and protagonists. Activist research is a tool for "creating the conditions we describe." We engage in the process of co-research to explore existing alternatives and possibilities for social change.

Anthropology and Social Change
anth@ciis.edu
1453 Mission Street
94103
San Francisco, California
www.ciis.edu/academics/graduate-programs/anthropology-and-social-change

Witches, Witch-Hunting, and Women

Silvia Federici

ISBN: 978-1-62963-568-2
$14.00   120 pages

We are witnessing a new surge of interpersonal and institutional violence against women, including new witch hunts. This surge of violence has occurred alongside an expansion of capitalist social relations. In this new work that revisits some of the main themes of *Caliban and the Witch*, Silvia Federici examines the root causes of these developments and outlines the consequences for the women affected and their communities. She argues that, no less than the witch hunts in sixteenth- and seventeenth-century Europe and the "New World," this new war on women is a structural element of the new forms of capitalist accumulation. These processes are founded on the destruction of people's most basic means of reproduction. Like at the dawn of capitalism, what we discover behind today's violence against women are processes of enclosure, land dispossession, and the remolding of women's reproductive activities and subjectivity.

As well as an investigation into the causes of this new violence, the book is also a feminist call to arms. Federici's work provides new ways of understanding the methods in which women are resisting victimization and offers a powerful reminder that reconstructing the memory of the past is crucial for the struggles of the present.

"It is good to think with Silvia Federici, whose clarity of analysis and passionate vision come through in essays that chronicle enclosure and dispossession, witch-hunting and other assaults against women, in the present, no less than the past. It is even better to act armed with her insights."
—Eileen Boris, Hull Professor of Feminist Studies, University of California, Santa Barbara

"Silvia Federici's new book offers a brilliant analysis and forceful denunciation of the violence directed towards women and their communities. Her focus moves between women criminalized as witches both at the dawn of capitalism and in contemporary globalization. Federici has updated the material from her well-known book Caliban and the Witch *and brings a spotlight to the current resistance and alternatives being pursued by women and their communities through struggle."*
—Massimo De Angelis, professor of political economy, University of East London

Re-enchanting the World: Feminism and the Politics of the Commons

Silvia Federici with a Foreword by Peter Linebaugh

ISBN: 978-1-62963-569-9
$19.95   240 pages

Silvia Federici is one of the most important contemporary theorists of capitalism and feminist movements. In this collection of her work spanning over twenty years, she provides a detailed history and critique of the politics of the commons from a feminist perspective. In her clear and combative voice, Federici provides readers with an analysis of some of the key issues and debates in contemporary thinking on this subject.

Drawing on rich historical research, she maps the connections between the previous forms of enclosure that occurred with the birth of capitalism and the destruction of the commons and the "new enclosures" at the heart of the present phase of global capitalist accumulation. Considering the commons from a feminist perspective, this collection centers on women and reproductive work as crucial to both our economic survival and the construction of a world free from the hierarchies and divisions capital has planted in the body of the world proletariat. Federici is clear that the commons should not be understood as happy islands in a sea of exploitative relations but rather autonomous spaces from which to challenge the existing capitalist organization of life and labor.

"Silvia Federici's theoretical capacity to articulate the plurality that fuels the contemporary movement of women in struggle provides a true toolbox for building bridges between different features and different people."
—Massimo De Angelis, professor of political economy, University of East London

"Silvia Federici's work embodies an energy that urges us to rejuvenate struggles against all types of exploitation and, precisely for that reason, her work produces a common: a common sense of the dissidence that creates a community in struggle."
—Maria Mies, coauthor of Ecofeminism